35 knitted baby blankets

for the nursery, stroller, and playtime

laura strutt

CICO BOOKS
LONDON NEW YORK

To my wonderful tribe of nieces and nephews: George, Henry, Miles, Charlotte, Becky, Charlie, Ella, Harvey, Alice, Harry, James, Thomas, Henry, and Hannah—many of whom I've been lucky enough to have knitted new baby gifts for!

SLEEP SAFETY NOTE: Keep your baby's head uncovered. Their blanket should be tucked in no higher than their shoulders. Don't let your baby get too hot or too cold. For further up-to-date advice on sleep safety, please talk to your healthcare provider. Neither the author nor the publisher can be held responsible for any claim arising out of the use or misuse of items or suggestions made in this book.

Published in 2016 by CICO Books
An imprint of Ryland Peters & Small Ltd
20–21 Jockey's Fields, London WC1R 4BW
341 E 116th St, New York, NY 10029

www.rylandpeters.com

10 9 8 7 6 5 4 3 2 1

A CIP catalog record for this book is available from the Library of Congress and the British Library.

ISBN: 978 1 78249 368 6

Printed in China

Editor: Rachel Atkinson
Pattern checker: Jemima Bicknell
Designer: Alison Fenton
Photographer: Holly Jolliffe
Stylist: Rob Merrett

Art director: Sally Powell
Production controller: Mai-Ling Collyer
Publishing manager: Penny Craig
Publisher: Cindy Richards

35 knitted baby blankets

contents

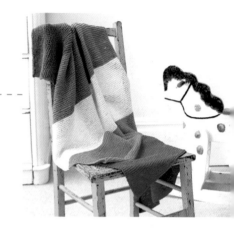

introduction

Like many people, I first learnt to knit when I was a small child taught by my mother and grandmother, but the interest in creating things with yarn and needles never really stuck. It wasn't until we were waiting on the arrival of my very first nephew that I decided to take up the needles again. After all, there is really no warmer welcome for a new baby than a super soft, cozy, hand-knitted blanket!

Working on baby knits is such a great way for beginners to build their confidence in knitting, allowing them to work on a wide range of different designs, using a selection of stitches and techniques, and the smaller scale of the projects makes them much more manageable. Seasoned knitters will enjoy building their skills with the more complex makes and fresh ideas for babies and children.

There is nothing more satisfying than knitting something for a new baby—aside from snuggling a new baby, of course— whether you are creating a gift to be treasured, something to welcome your own new addition, or even to donate to a local neo-natal hospital unit or charity—there are plenty of ideas and designs in this collection for newborns through to toddlers.

It was such a great joy to design and create the projects in this book, mixing different stitches and techniques, working with both classic and more contemporary color and yarn combinations to create this collection of knitted baby blankets. I hope that you have just as much fun making them and wrapping the little ones in your life in a handmade hug!

Happy knitting!

Laura

Note: Each project includes a star rating as a skill level guide and you will find the project includes the techniques listed below:
★ Suitable for new knitters using basic stitches with minimal shaping.
★★ Repetitive stitch patterns, simple color changes, and basic lace patterns with simple shaping and finishing.
★★★ Stranded colorwork, intarsia, complex lace patterns with mid-level shaping and finishing.

chapter 1   nursery

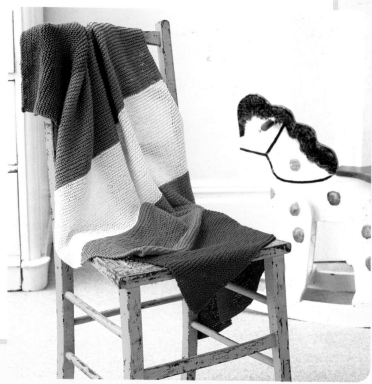

love heart motif

Show your love with a heart motif blanket. This intarsia design worked in cream and red, makes a lovely gift for new babies.

Materials
- Red Heart Soft worsted (aran) weight yarn (100% acrylic; 183yds/167m per 3½oz/100g ball)
  2 balls of shade 002 Cream (A)
  1 ball of shade 004 Wine Red (B)
- US 8 (5mm) knitting needles
- 2 stitch markers
- Tapestry needle

Finished Measurements
19in (48cm) x 25in (64cm)

Gauge (Tension)
17 sts and 24 rows to measure 4in (10cm) over stockinette (stocking) stitch on US 8 (5mm) needles after blocking

Abbreviations
See page 127.

Special Stitch
sl2, k1, p2sso: Slip 2 stitches together knitwise, knit the next stitch, then pass the 2 slipped stitches over this knitted stitch to decrease 2 stitches.

heart motif chart

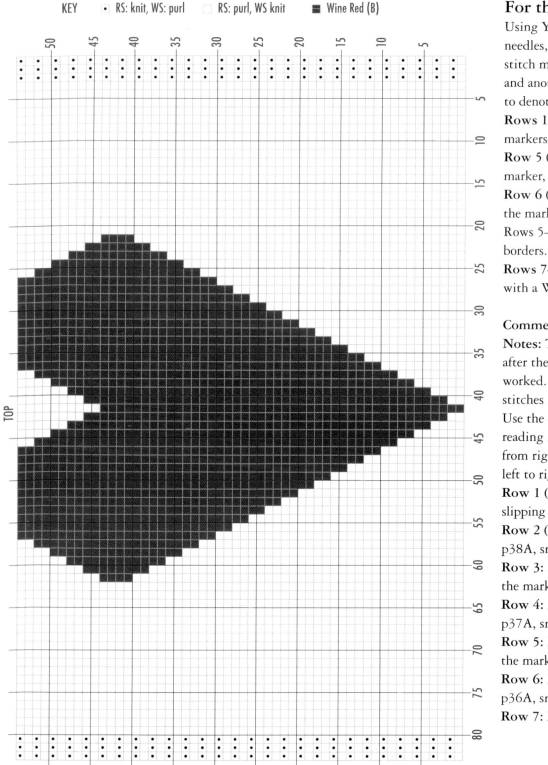

For the Blanket

Using Yarn A and US 8 (5mm) needles, cast on 83 sts placing a stitch marker between sts 3 and 4 and another between sts 80 and 81 to denote the border.

Rows 1–4: Knit to end, slipping the markers as you pass them.

Row 5 (WS): K3, sm, p to next marker, sm, k3.

Row 6 (RS): Knit to end, slipping the markers as you pass them.

Rows 5–6 set St st and garter st borders.

Rows 7–45: Rep rows 5–6, ending with a WS row.

Commence Heart Motif

Notes: The yarn color used is given after the number of stitches to be worked. For example: K5A = knit 5 stitches in Yarn A.

Use the chart for reference if desired, reading it from bottom to top and from right to left on RS rows, and left to right on WS rows.

Row 1 (RS): K41A, k1B, k41A, slipping the markers as you pass them.

Row 2 (WS): K3A, sm, p38A, p1B, p38A, sm, k3A.

Row 3: K40A, k3B, k40A, slipping the markers as you pass them.

Row 4: K3A, sm, p37A, p3B, p37A, sm, k3A.

Row 5: K39A, k5B, k39A, slipping the markers as you pass them.

Row 6: K3A, sm, p36A, p5B, p36A, sm, k3A.

Row 7: K38A, k7B, k38A, slipping

the markers as you pass them.

Row 8: K3A, sm, p35A, p7B, p35A, sm, k3A.

Row 9: K37A, k9B, k37A, slipping the markers as you pass them.

Row 10: K3A, sm, p34A, p9B, p34A, sm, k3A.

Row 11: K36A, k11B, k36A, slipping the markers as you pass them.

Row 12: K3A, sm, p33A, p11B, p33A, sm, k3A.

Row 13: K35A, k13B, k35A, slipping the markers as you pass them.

Row 14: K3A, sm, p32A, p13B, p32A, sm, k3A.

Row 15: K34A, k15B, k34A, slipping the markers as you pass them.

Row 16: K3A, sm, p31A, p15B, p31A, sm, k3A.

Row 17: K33A, k17B, k33A, slipping the markers as you pass them.

Row 18: K3A, sm, p30A, p17B, p30A, sm, k3A.

Row 19: K32A, k19B, k32A, slipping the markers as you pass them.

Row 20: K3A, sm, p29A, p19B, p29A, sm, k3A.

Row 21: K31A, k21B, k31A, slipping the markers as you pass them.

Row 22: K3A, sm, p28A, p21B, p28A, sm, k3A.

Row 23: K30A, k23B, k30A, slipping the markers as you pass them.

Row 24: K3A, sm, p27A, p23B, p27A, sm, k3A.

Row 25: K29A, k25A, k29A, slipping the markers as you pass them.

Row 26: K3A, sm, p26A, p25B, p26A, sm, k3A.

Row 27: K28A, k27B, k28A, slipping the markers as you pass them.

Row 28: K3A, sm, p25A, p27B, p25A, sm, k3A.

Row 29: K27A, k29B, k27A, slipping the markers as you pass them.

Row 30: K3A, sm, p24A, p29B, p24A, sm, k3A.

Row 31: K26A, k31B, k26A, slipping the markers as you pass them.

Row 32: K3A, sm, p23, p31B, p23A, sm, k3A.

Row 33: K25A, k33B, k25A, slipping the

markers as you pass them.

Row 34: K3A, sm, p22A, p33B, p22A, sm, k3A.

Row 35: K24A, k35B, k24A, slipping the markers as you pass them.

Row 36: K3A, sm, p21A, p35B, p21A, sm, k3A.

Row 37: K23A, k37B, k23A, slipping the markers as you pass them.

Row 38: K3A, sm, p20A, p37B, p20A, sm, k3A.

Row 39: K22A, k39B, k22A, slipping the markers as you pass them.

Row 40: K3A, sm, p19A, p39B, p19A, sm, k3A.

Row 41: K21A, k41B, k21A, slipping the markers as you pass them.

Row 42: K3A, sm, p18A, p41B, p18A, sm, k3A.

Row 43: K21A, k41B, k21A, slipping the markers as you pass them.

Row 44: K3A, sm, p18A, p41B, p18A, sm, k3A.

Row 45: K22A, k19B, k1A, k19B, k22A, slipping the markers as you pass them.

Row 46: K3A, sm, p19A, p19B, p1A, p19B, p19A, sm, k3A.

Row 47: K23A, k17B, k3A, k17B, k23A, slipping the markers as you pass them.

Row 48: K3A, sm, p20A, p17B, p3A, p17B, p20A, sm, k3A.

Row 49: K24A, k15B, k5A, k15B, k24A, slipping the markers as you pass them.

Row 50: K3A, sm, p21A, p15B, p5A, p15B, p21A, sm, k3A.

Row 51: K25A, k13B, k7A, k13B, k25A, slipping the markers as you pass them.

Row 52: K3A, sm, p22A, p13B, p7A, p13B, p22A, sm, k3A.

Row 53: K26A, k11B, k9A, k11B, k26A, slipping the markers as you pass them.

Row 54: K3A, sm, p23A, p11B, p9A, p11B, p23A, sm, k3A.

Break Yarn B and continue in Yarn A only.

Row 1: Knit.

Row 2: K3, sm, p to next marker, sm, k3.

Rows 1–2 set St st and garter st borders.

Rows 3–41: Rep rows 1–2, ending with a RS row.

Next 4 rows: Knit, removing the markers (sm) as you pass them.

Bind (cast) off knitwise.

Making Up and Finishing

Weave in all loose ends and block to measurements.

colorblock afghan

skill rating
★☆☆

Bright colors and simple garter stitch combine to make this
cheerful easy-knit baby afghan. Worked in wonderfully soft cotton
yarn, it has a luxurious drape and is completely reversible too.

make it yours

Create an ombré effect afghan by working with a selection of varying shades of the same color.

Materials

- Cascade Ultra Pima light worsted (DK) weight yarn (100% cotton; 220yds/200m per 3½oz/100g ball)

  1 ball of shade 3774 Major Teal (A)

  1 ball of shade 3726 Periwinkle (B)

  1 ball of shade 3718 Natural (C)

  1 ball of shade 3767 Deep Coral (D)

  1 ball of shade 3702 Pink Sapphire (E)

- US 6 (4mm) knitting needles—24–32in (60–80cm) circular needles are recommended due to the number of stitches, but long straight needles can be used if preferred

- Tapestry needle

Finished Measurements

28½in (74cm) x 40in (100cm)

Gauge (Tension)

21 sts x 33 rows to measure 4in (10cm) over garter stitch on US 6 (4mm) needles after blocking

Abbreviations

See page 127.

For the Afghan

Using Yarn A and US 6 (4mm) needles, cast on 150 sts.

Row 1: Knit.

Row 2: Knit.

Rows 1–2 set garter st pattern.

Work a further 64 rows in garter st.

Row 67: Change to Yarn B and work 66 rows in garter st.

Row 133: Change to Yarn C and work 66 rows in garter st.

Row 199: Change to Yarn D and work 66 rows in garter st.

Row 265: Change to Yarn E and work 66 rows in garter st, ending on row 330.

Bind (cast) off.

Making Up and Finishing

Weave in all loose ends and block to measurements.

honeycomb afghan

This clever design uses slip stitches to create an afghan that looks multi-dimensional, and worked in yellow and gray yarns it grows into a sweet honeycomb motif.

Materials
- Berroco Vintage worsted (aran) weight yarn (52% acrylic/40% wool/8% nylon; 207yds/198m per 3½oz/100g ball)
  1 ball of shade 5106 Smoke (A)
  2 balls of shade 5121 Sunny (B)
- US 8 (5mm) knitting needles
- Tapestry needle

Finished Measurements
19¼in (49cm) x 21½in (55cm)

Gauge (Tension)
16 sts x 24 rows to measure 4in (10cm) over stockinette (stocking) stitch on US 8 (5mm) needles after blocking

Abbreviations
See page 127.

Pattern Notes
Ensure that all slip stitches are slipped purlwise to maintain a consistent finish on the afghan after blocking.

tip
No need to cut the yarns as you finish each row; loosely carry the unused yarn at the side of the work by catching it under the working yarn as you make the first stitch, this will ensure that the yarns are always in the correct place as you work through the pattern repeats.

For the Afghan
Using Yarn A and US 8 (5mm) needles, cast on 84 sts.
Rows 1–2: Knit.
Row 3: Change to Yarn B. Knit.
Rows 4–5: Change to Yarn A. Knit.
Row 6 (RS): Change to Yarn B. K1, sl next 2 sts purlwise, *k6, sl next 2 sts purlwise; rep from * to last st, k1.
Row 7 (WS): P1, sl next 2 sts purlwise, *p6, sl next 2 sts purlwise; rep from * to last st, p1.
Row 8: K1, sl next 2 sts purlwise, *k6, sl next 2 sts purlwise; rep from * to last st, k1.
Rows 9–10: Rep Rows 7–8.
Row 11: Rep Row 7.
Rows 12–13: Change to Yarn A. Knit.
Row 14: Change to Yarn B. K5, sl next 2 sts purlwise, *k6, sl next 2 sts purlwise; rep from * to last 5 sts, k5.
Row 15: P5, sl next 2 sts purlwise, *p6, sl next 2 sts purlwise; rep from * to last 5 sts, p5.
Rows 16–19: Rep Rows 14–15 twice.
Rows 20–21: Change to Yarn A. Knit.
Rep Rows 6–21 a further 9 times.
Next row: Change to Yarn B. Knit.
Next 2 rows: Change to Yarn A, knit.
Bind (cast) off.

For the Border
With RS facing, working down each side of the afghan in turn at the row ends, using Yarn A and US 8 (5mm) needles, pick up and k80 sts along the side of the afghan.

Rows 1–2: Knit.

Row 3: Change to Yarn B. Knit.

Rows 4–5: Change to Yarn A. Knit.

Bind (cast) off.

Rep to add a border to the second side.

Making Up and Finishing

Using the yarn tail, sew the corners of the border together to make neat miters.

Weave in all loose ends and block to measurements.

newborn cocoon

Baby will be snug as a bug in this little cocoon, which is the perfect quick-make gift for newborns and an ideal accessory for those all important first photographs.

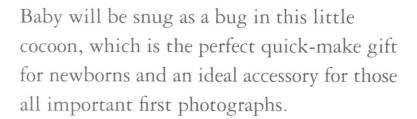

Materials
- Araucania Huasco light worsted (DK) weight yarn (100% wool; 306yds/280m per 3½oz/100g skein) 1 skein of shade 402
- US 6 (4mm) circular needle, 24in (60cm) length
- US 6 (4mm) double-pointed needles (DPNs), 8in (20cm) length—set of 5 needles
- Stitch marker
- Tapestry needle

Finished Measurements
20in (51cm) circumference x 15½in (39cm) long

Gauge (Tension)
21 sts x 36 rows to measure 4in (10cm) over stockinette (stocking) stitch worked in the round on US 6 (4mm) needles after blocking

Abbreviations
See page 127.

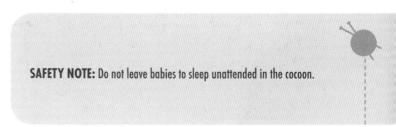

SAFETY NOTE: Do not leave babies to sleep unattended in the cocoon.

For the Cocoon
Using US 6 (4mm) circular needle, cast on 100 sts. Join for working in the round, taking care not to twist the sts and place a stitch marker to indicate beginning of round. Knit every round until work measures 13in (33cm) from cast-on edge.

For the Base
Change to DPNs, evenly distributing the sts onto 4 needles (25 sts on each needle) and using the fifth needle to work with, continue as follows:
Round 1: [Ssk, k21, k2tog] 4 times. (92 sts)
Round 2: Knit.
Round 3: [Ssk, k19, k2tog] 4 times. (84 sts)
Round 4: Knit.
Round 5: [Ssk, k17, k2tog] 4 times. (76 sts)
Round 6: Knit.
Round 7: [Ssk, k15, k2tog] 4 times. (68 sts)
Round 8: Knit.
Round 9: [Ssk, k13, k2tog] 4 times. (60 sts)
Round 10: Knit.
Round 11: [Ssk, k11, k2tog] 4 times. (52 sts)
Round 12: Knit.
Round 13: [Ssk, k9, k2tog] 4 times. (44 sts)
Round 14: Knit.
Round 15: [Ssk, k7, k2tog] 4 times. (36 sts)
Round 16: Knit.
Round 17: [Ssk, k5, k2tog] 4 times. (28 sts)
Round 18: Knit.
Round 19: [Ssk, k3, k2tog] 4 times. (20 sts)
Round 20: Knit.
Divide the remaining sts over two needles and graft the ends closed using Kitchener st.

Making Up and Finishing
Weave in all loose ends and block to measurements.

make it yours
Increase the width or length of the cocoon by casting on more stitches or working additional rows in stockinette (stocking) stitch before working the shaping at the base of the cocoon.

modern lace blanket

Linen yarns are spun from a wonderfully soft natural fiber that knits up to create a blanket with lots of drape. This light and floaty blanket is cool against the skin, making it ideal for spring or summer babies and is a great project for knitters looking to learn the next stage of lace knitting.

Materials
- Rowan Pure Linen worsted (aran) weight yarn (100% linen; 142yds/130m per 1¾oz/50g ball) 3 balls of shade 388 Arctic
- US 8 (5mm) knitting needles
- 2 stitch markers
- Tapestry needle

Finished Measurements
33in (84cm) wide x 26in (66cm) long

Gauge (Tension)
14 sts x 24 rows to measure 4in (10cm) over lace pattern on US 8 (5mm) needles after blocking

Abbreviations
See page 127.

Special Stitch
sl2, k1, p2sso: Slip 2 stitches together knitwise, knit the next stitch, then pass the 2 slipped stitches over this knitted stitch to decrease 2 stitches.

For the Blanket

Using US 8 (5mm) needles, cast on 111 sts placing a stitch marker between sts 3 and 4 and another between sts 108 and 109.

Rows 1–3: Knit to end, slipping the markers (sm) as you pass them.

Row 4 (WS): K3, sm, p to next marker, sm, k3.

Row 5 (RS): K3, sm, k2, *yo, ssk, k6; rep from * to last 10 sts, yo, ssk, k5, sm, k3.

Row 6: K3, sm, p to next marker, sm, k3.

Row 7: K3, sm, k3, *yo, ssk, k3, k2tog, yo, k1; rep from * to last 9 sts, yo, ssk, k4, sm, k3.

Row 8: K3, sm, p to next marker, sm, k3.

Row 9: K3, sm, k4, *yo, ssk, k1, k2tog, yo, k3; rep from * to last 8 sts, yo, ssk, k3, sm, k3.

Row 10: K3, sm, p to next marker, sm, k3.

Row 11: K3, sm, k2, k2tog, *yo, k5, yo, sl2, k1, p2sso; rep from * to last 8 sts, yo, k5, sm, k3.

Row 12: K3, sm, p to next marker, sm, k3.

Row 13: K3, sm, k6, *yo, ssk, k6; rep from * to last 6 sts, yo, ssk, k1, sm, k3.

Row 14: K3, sm, p to next marker, sm, k3.

Row 15: K3, sm, k4, k2tog, *yo, k1, yo, ssk, k3, k2tog; rep from * to last 6 sts, yo, k3, sm, k3.

Row 16: K3, sm, p to next marker, sm, k3.

Row 17: K3, sm, k3, *k2tog, yo, k3, yo, ssk, k1; rep from * to last 9 sts, k2tog, yo, k4, sm, k3.

Row 18: K3, sm, p to next marker, sm, k3.

Row 19: K3, sm, k5, *yo, sl2, k1, p2sso, yo, k5; rep from * to last 7sts, yo, k2tog, k2, sm, k3.

Rep Rows 4–19 a further 9 times. (10 repeats worked in total) ending on row 147.

Next 3 rows: Knit to end, slipping the markers as you pass them.

Bind (cast) off knitwise.

Making Up and Finishing

Weave in all loose ends and block firmly to measurements to open up the lace pattern.

tips

The stitch markers placed three stitches in from each end of the row are there to remind you to work these stitches in garter stitch pattern for the border.

Linen yarn can be quite slippery to work with and it is also easy to put your needle through the strand and miss some of the plies. You may therefore find it easier to work with a blunter bamboo needle when knitting linen yarn.

make it yours

Linen yarns are also available in wonderfully vibrant shades—pick a bold color for a more striking blanket.

chunky snuggle comforter

This bold and chunky knit makes a great comforter for little ones and the soft dense stitches will keep them nice and cozy during colder nights.

Materials
- Debbie Bliss Rialto Chunky bulky (chunky) weight yarn (100% wool; 66yds/60m per 1¾oz/50g ball) 9 balls of shade 007 Gold
- US 10½ (6.5mm) knitting needles
- Tapestry needle

Finished Measurements
30in (76cm) square

Gauge (Tension)
14 sts x 22 rows to measure 4in (10cm) over stockinette (stocking) stitch on US 10½ (6.5mm) needles after blocking

Abbreviations
See page 127.

For the Comforter

Using US 10½ (6.5mm) needles, cast on 103 sts.

Row 1 (RS): [K1, p1] to last st, k1.

Row 2 (WS): [P1, k1] to last st, p1.

Rows 3–4: Rep Rows 1–2.

Row 5: Knit.

Row 6: Purl.

Rep Rows 5–6 until work measures 29in (74.5cm) from cast-on edge.

Rep Rows 1–4 once more.

Bind (cast) off.

For the Side Borders

With RS facing, pick up and k87 sts along one row-end edge of the blanket.

Rep Rows 1–4.

Bind (cast) off.

Rep to add border to opposite side.

Making Up and Finishing

Weave in all loose ends and block to measurements.

make it yours

The simple nature of this comforter makes it a great blank canvas for adding your own personal touch—add in stripes or work a contrast color border.

bunting blanket

skill rating
★★☆

Add a flash of brightly colored bunting-style edging to create this knit. These mini-pennant edgings are the perfect way to use up any odds and ends in your stash.

make it yours

Match the colors of the bunting to work stripes across the blanket for an even more colorful finish.

Materials

- Rowan Cotton Glace light worsted (DK) weight yarn (100% cotton; 126yds/115m per 1¾oz/50g ball)

  4 balls of shade 725 Ecru (A)

  1 ball of shade 741 Poppy (B)

  1 ball of shade 856 Mineral (C)

  1 ball of shade 850 Cobalt (D)

  1 ball of shade 861 Rose (E)

  1 ball of shade 832 Persimmon (F)

  1 ball of shade 858 Aqua (G)

  1 ball of shade 868 Midnight (H)

  1 ball of shade 864 Greengage (I)

- US 6 (4mm) knitting needles
- Tapestry needle

Finished Measurements

20in (51cm) square

Gauge (Tension)

20 sts and 36 rows to measure 4in (10cm) over garter stitch on US 6 (4mm) needles after blocking

Abbreviations

See page 127.

For the Blanket

Using Yarn A and US 6 (4mm) needles, cast on 80 sts.
Knit every row until work measures 16in (41cm) from cast-on edge.
Bind (cast) off knitwise.

For the Border

** Using Yarn G and US 6 (4mm) needles, pick up and k80 sts along one side.

Row 1: Knit.

Row 2: Change to Yarn C. Knit.

Row 3: Knit.

Row 4: Change to Yarn G. Knit.

Bind (cast) off knitwise.

Rep from ** to add a border to each of the three other sides.
Stitch the border edges together at the corner.

For the Bunting Edging

Using Yarn D and US 6 (4mm) needles, beginning 1 st from any corner, pick up and k10 sts along the edge of the blanket.

Row 1: Knit.

Row 2: K2tog, k to last 2 sts, k2tog. (8 sts)

Row 3: Knit.

Row 4: K2tog, k to last 2 sts, k2tog. (6 sts)

Row 5: Knit.

Row 6: K2tog, k to last 2 sts, k2tog. (4 sts)

Row 7: Knit.

Row 8: [K2tog] twice. (2 sts)

Row 9: Knit.

Row 10: K2tog. (1 st)

Break yarn and pull through remaining st to fasten off. (First bunting pennant completed)
Skip 1 st of side, then, using Yarn I, pick up another 10 sts along side and rep Rows 1–10 to make a second bunting pennant.
Continue working bunting pennants as set along this side, working pennants in colors F, E, H, C, B.
Rep this section for each remaining side.

Making Up and Finishing

Weave in all loose ends and block to measurements, taking care to pin-out the points of each bunting pennant.

tip

When working the border, carry the yarn not in use loosely up the side to save cutting and rejoining it after each color change.

corner-to-corner blanket

This blanket is knitted from one corner to the opposite with the shape created by increasing and then decreasing in turn to form a square. Alternating yarns every few rows creates vibrant diagonal stripes and a fully reversible design.

Materials
- Bernat Cotton-ish Vintage light worsted (DK) weight yarn (55% cotton/45% acrylic; 282yds/ 258m per 2½oz/70g ball)
  1 ball of shade 85044 Grey T-Shirt (A)
  1 ball of shade 85315 Cotton Gin (B)
- US 7 (4.5mm) knitting needles
- Tapestry needle

Finished Measurements
23in (59cm) square

Gauge (Tension)
20 sts x 32 rows to measure 4in (10cm) over garter stitch on US 7 (4.5mm) needles after blocking

Abbreviations
See page 127.

tips

The yarnovers (yo) are used to increase the stitch count throughout the first half of the pattern and as a decorative feature on the second part when the design is decreasing. Take care to ensure you work these on every alternate row throughout the blanket.

This pattern is suitable for adventurous beginners looking to build skills—regularly checking stitch counts will help keep you on track.

For the Blanket

Using Yarn A and US 7 (4.5mm) needles, cast on 6 sts.
Row 1: Knit.
Row 2: K2, yo, k2, yo, k2. (8 sts)
Row 3: Knit.
Row 4: K2, yo, k4, yo, k2. (10 sts)
Row 5: Knit.
Row 6: K2, yo, k6, yo, k2. (12 sts)
Row 7: Knit.
Row 8: K2, yo, k to last 2 sts, yo, k2. (2 sts increased)
Change to Yarn B and rep Rows 7–8 a further 4 times.
(8 rows worked in stripes, 8 sts increased—22 sts total)

Change to yarn A and rep Rows 7–8 a further 4 times. (30 sts)

Continue increasing in stripe pattern as set to 142 sts (you will have completed your seventeenth stripe, which will be in Yarn A). Continuing with Yarn A, rep Rows 7–8 once more (seventeenth stripe will have 10 rows). (144 sts)

Change to Yarn B and commence decreases as follows:

Next row: K3, k2tog, k to last 5 sts, k2tog, k3. (2 sts decreased)

Next row: K2, yo, k2tog, k to last 4 sts, k2tog, yo, k2. Rep last 2 rows a further 4 times (eighteenth stripe will

have 10 rows). (134 sts)

Change to Yarn A and rep last 2 rows a further 4 times. Continue as set, changing yarns every 8 rows and decreasing 2 sts every alternate row until 6 sts remain. Bind (cast) off knitwise.

Making Up and Finishing

Weave in all loose ends and block carefully to a square.

hi blanket

What better way to welcome a new arrival than with a sweet greeting blanket? Use the neat duplicate stitch (Swiss darning) method to add your own message and create a gift that is sure to be treasured!

Materials
- Debbie Bliss Cashmerino Aran worsted weight yarn (55% wool/33% acrylic/12% cashmere; 98yds/90m per 1¾oz/50g ball)
  3 balls of shade 101 Ecru (A)
  1 ball of shade 009 Grey (B)
- US 8 (5mm) knitting needles
- US G/6 (4mm) crochet hook
- Pins
- Tapestry needle

Finished Measurements
17½in (44.5cm) x 20in (51cm)

Gauge (Tension)
16 sts x 24 rows to measure 4in (10cm) over stockinette (stocking) stitch on US 8 (5mm) needles after blocking

Abbreviations
See page 127.

tips

Maintain an even stitch length when working the duplicate stitch to ensure that the "Hi" motif is neat.

When working duplicate stitch, try working the design up and down, rather than across the rows—this will create a more professional finish.

For the Blanket
Using Yarn A and US 8 (5mm) needles, cast on 72 sts.
Rows 1–3: *K1, p1; rep from * to end.
Row 4 (RS): Knit.
Row 5 (WS): Purl.
Rows 6–113: Rep Rows 4–5.
Rows 114–116: *K1, p1; rep from * to end.
Bind (cast) off knitwise.

For the Crocheted Border
Note: US single crochet (sc) = UK double crochet (dc).
Using Yarn B and US G/6 (4mm) crochet hook, join yarn in one side edge and work 1ch, then 1sc in each row end and stitch around working [1sc, 1ch, 1sc] in each corner.

For the Duplicate Stitch Hi Motif
Block blanket to measurements (blocking before working the motif will give a more even fabric to work the duplicate stitch into).
Use the pins to mark out a central rectangle of stitches measuring 15 stitches by 30 rows.
Follow the chart, working duplicate stitch (see page 125) over each marked stitch in B.

hi blanket chart

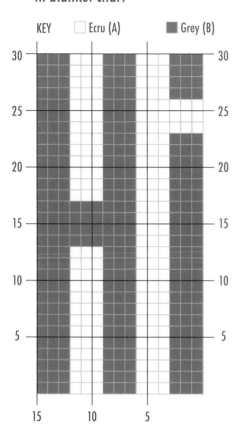

KEY   ☐ Ecru (A)   ■ Grey (B)

Making Up and Finishing

Weave in all loose ends and block again to measurements if desired.

textured squares

Combine a simple pattern of knit and purl stitches to create a tactile design with textured squares that is fully reversible.

Materials
- Mirasol Pima Kuri light worsted (DK) weight yarn (100% cotton; 208yds/190m per 3½oz/100g ball) 2 balls of shade 11 Darling Lilac
- US 7 (4.5mm) knitting needles
- 2 stitch markers
- Tapestry needle

Finished Measurements
21¼in (54cm) x 23½in (60cm)

Gauge (Tension)
20 sts x 27 rows to measure 4in (10cm) over stockinette (stocking) stitch on US 7 (4.5mm) needles after blocking

Abbreviations
See page 127.

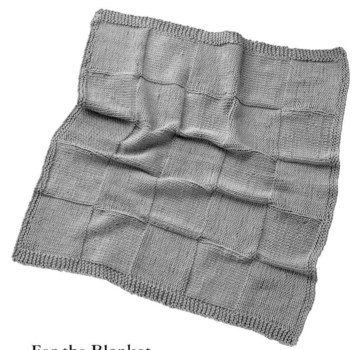

tips

This pattern uses stitch markers to indicate the five stitches at each end of the row—these stitches are worked as knit on both sides to create a garter stitch border.

There is no right side or wrong side for this blanket—it is fully reversible so take the time to weave in all the yarn ends carefully.

For the Blanket
Using US 7 (4.5mm) needles, cast on 110 sts.
Row 1: K5, pm, k100, pm, k5.
Row 2: K5, sm, k to marker, sm, k5.
Rows 3–5: Rep Row 2.
Row 6: K5, sm, [k20, p20] twice, k20, sm, k5.
Row 7: K5, sm, [p20, k20] twice, p20, sm, k5.
Rows 8–33: Rep Rows 6–7.
Row 34: K5, sm, [p20, k20] twice, p20, sm, k5.
Row 35: K5, sm, [k20, p20] twice, k20, sm, k5.
Rows 36–61: Rep Rows 34–35.
Row 62: K5, sm, [k20, p20] twice, k20, sm, k5.
Row 63: K5, sm, [p20, k20] twice, p20, sm, k5.
Rows 64–89: Rep Rows 62–63.

make it yours

To make the pattern really stand out why not add a seed (moss) stitch border for the first and last five rows, and for the first and last five stitches on each row, instead of garter stitch?

Row 90: K5, sm, [p20, k20] twice, p20, sm, k5.
Row 91: K5, sm, [k20, p20] twice, k20, sm, k5.
Rows 92–117: Rep Rows 90–91.
Row 118: K5, sm, [k20, p20] twice, k20, sm, k5.
Row 119: K5, sm, [p20, k20] twice, p20, sm, k5.
Rows 120–145: Rep Rows 118–119.
Rows 146–150: Knit to end, removing markers as you pass them.
Bind (cast) off knitwise.

Making Up and Finishing

Weave in all loose ends and block to measurements.

dungaree cozy

Keep baby snug and warm with this adorable dungaree cozy made with soft merino yarn. The simple straps and button placement can be adjusted to fit baby perfectly.

make it yours

The super simple shaping of the lower portion makes the perfect blank canvas for some customization—why not add in a colorwork motif or some stripes?

Materials
- MillaMia Naturally Soft Merino fingering (4ply) weight yarn (100% wool; 136yds/125m per 1¾oz/50g ball)
  3 balls of shade 161 Seaside (A)
  1 ball of shade 102 Storm (B)
- US 7 (4.5mm) circular needle, 24in (60cm) length
- US 3 (3.25mm) circular needle, 16in (40cm) length
- Stitch marker
- 2 buttons, 1¼in (3cm) diameter
- Tapestry needle

Finished Measurements
18in (46cm) to the top of the dungaree section, 13in (33cm) wide

Gauge (Tension)
22 sts x 32 rows to measure 4in (10cm) over stockinette (stocking) stitch on US 7 (4.5mm) needles after blocking

Abbreviations
See page 127.

For the Base

Using Yarn A and US 7 (4.5mm) needles, cast on 140 sts. Join for working in the round and place stitch marker to indicate beginning of round.

Knit every round until work measures 15in (38cm).

Next round (Dec): *K12, k2tog; rep from * to end. (130 sts)

Next round: Knit.

Next round (Dec): *K11, k2tog; rep from * to end. (120 sts)

Change to Yarn B and US 3 (3.25mm) needles.

Next round (Rib): *K1, p1; rep from * to end. Work 22 rounds in Rib as set.

Next round (Buttonholes): Rib 13 sts, *bring yarn to front between the needles, sl next st purlwise, take yarn back between needles to wrap the st, {sl next st purlwise, pass first sl st over} 3 times, turn work, cable cast on 4 sts, turn work, place last cast-on st on left needle, bring yarn to front between needles, slip st back to right needle, take yarn back between needles to wrap st, sl next st knitwise and pass last cast-on st over to complete the buttonhole*, rib 24 sts, rep from * to * once more, rib to end. Work 5 rounds in Rib as set.

Bind (cast) off in Rib.

For the Straps (make 2 alike)

Using Yarn B and US 3 (3.25mm) needles, cast on 10 sts.

Knit every row for 8in (20cm).

Bind (cast) off.

Making Up and Finishing

Weave in all loose ends and block to measurements. Seam the base of the sleep bag using **Yarn A** and mattress stitch (see page 124).

Align the straps with the buttonholes and sew securely onto the back of the dungaree section with mattress stitch. Securely sew the buttons on straps to correspond with the buttonholes.

overlapping waves lace

skill rating
★★☆

This delicate lace stitch makes a pretty and lightweight cover up, ideal for summer babies.

Materials
- Debbie Bliss Luxury Silk light worsted (DK) weight yarn (100% silk; 109yds/100m per 1¾oz/ 50g ball)
  2 balls of shade 042 Spice
- US 8 (5mm) knitting needles
- Tapestry needle

Finished Measurements
17¾in (45cm) wide x 23in (58cm) long

Gauge (Tension)
14 sts x 21 rows to measure 4in (10cm) over lace pattern on US 8 (5mm) needles after blocking

Abbreviations
See page 127.

make it yours

Work in a pale solid-colored yarn for a more traditional look.

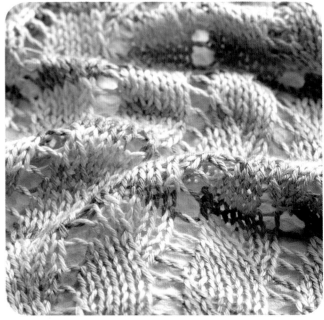

For the Blanket

Using US 8 (5mm) needles, cast on 72 sts.

Rows 1–3: Knit.

Row 4 (RS): K3, *yo, ssk, k4; rep from * to last 3 sts, yo, ssk, k1.

Row 5 (WS): K1, p to last st, k1.

Row 6: K3, *yo, k1, ssk, k3; rep from * to last 3 sts, yo, ssk, k1.

Row 7: K1, p to last st, k1.

Row 8: K3, *yo, k2, ssk, k2; rep from * to last 3 sts, yo, ssk, k1.

Row 9: K1, p to last st, k1.

Row 10: K3, *yo, k3, ssk, k1; rep from * to last 3 sts, yo, ssk, k1.

Row 11: K1, p to last st, k1.

Row 12: K3, *yo, k4, ssk; rep from * to last 3 sts, yo, ssk, k1.

Row 13: K1, p to last st, k1.

Rows 4–13 set the pattern.

Rep Rows 4–13 a further 10 times.

Next 3 rows: Knit.

Bind (cast) off knitwise.

Making Up and Finishing

Weave in loose ends and wet block firmly to measurements (see wet blocking page 123 step 2)—this blanket really benefits from firm blocking to open up the lace pattern.

tip

This is a great pattern for new lace knitters looking to improve their skills. Take care to keep track of the row just worked and insert a lifeline (see page 56) after checking that the stitch count and pattern is correct after every repeat—this will save having to rip back any mistakes.

textured triangles

skill rating
★☆☆

This striking textured blanket is created by working combinations of knit and purl stitches, making it a surprisingly simple, but highly effective blanket for new and experienced knitters.

Materials
- Brown Sheep Company Lamb's Pride worsted (aran) weight yarn (85% wool/15% mohair; 190yds/173m per 4oz/113g ball) 2 balls of shade M16 Seafoam
- US 8 (5mm) knitting needles
- 2 stitch markers
- Tapestry needle

Finished Measurements
21¼in (54cm) wide x 25in (63.5cm) long

Gauge (Tension)
17 sts x 24 rows to measure 4in (10cm) over stockinette (stocking) stitch on US 8 (5mm) needles after blocking

Abbreviations
See page 127.

make it yours

Working in a variegated yarn or adding a contrast color to the border will give a unique finish to this blanket.

For the Blanket

Using US 8 (5mm) needles, cast on 89 sts.

Row 1 (RS): K2, pm, k to last 2 sts, pm, k2.

Row 2 (WS): K2, sm, k to marker, sm, k2.

Row 3: K2, sm, p6, *k1, p11; rep from * to last 9 sts, k1, p6, sm, k2.

Row 4: K2, sm, k6, *p1, k11; rep from * to last 9 sts, p1, k6, sm, k2.

Row 5: K2, sm, p5, *k3, p9; rep from * to last 10 sts, k3, p5, sm, k2.

Row 6: K2, sm, k5, *p3, k9; rep from * to last 10 sts, p3, k5, sm, k2.

Row 7: K2, sm, p4, *k5, p7; rep from * to last 11 sts, k5, p4, sm, k2.

Row 8: K2, sm, k4, *p5, k7; rep from * to last 11 sts, p5, k4, sm, k2.

Row 9: K2, sm, p3, *k7, p5; rep from * to last 12 sts, k7, p3, sm, k2.

Row 10: K2, sm, k3, *p7, k5; rep from * to last 12 sts, p7, k3, sm, k2.

Row 11: K2, sm, p2, *k9, p3; rep from * to last 13 sts, k9, p2, sm, k2.

Row 12: K2, sm, k2, *p9, k3; rep from * to last 13 sts, p9, k2, sm, k2.

Row 13: K2, sm, p1, *k11, p1; rep from * to last 2 sts, sm, k2.

Row 14: K2, sm, k1, *p11, k1; rep from * to last 2 sts, sm, k2.

Row 15: K2, sm, k1, *p11, k1; rep from * to last 2 sts, sm, k2.

Row 16: K2, sm, p1, *k11, p1; rep from * to last 2 sts, sm, k2.

Row 17: K2, sm, k2, *p9, k3; rep from * to last 13 sts, p9, k2, sm, k2.

Row 18: K2, sm, p2, *k9, p3; rep from * to last 13 sts, k9, p2, sm, k2.

Row 19: K2, sm, k3, *p7, k5; rep from * to last 12 sts, p7, k3, sm, k2.

Row 20: K2, sm, p3, *k7, p5; rep from * to last 12 sts, k7, p3, sm, k2.

Row 21: K2, sm, k4, *p5, k7; rep from * to last 11 sts, p5, k4, sm, k2.

Row 22: K2, sm, p4, *k5, p7; rep from * to last 11 sts, k5, p4, sm, k2.

Row 23: K2, sm, k5, *p3, k9; rep from * to last 10 sts, p3, k5, sm, k2.

Row 24: K2, sm, p5, *k3, p9; rep from * to last 10 sts, k3, p5, sm, k2.

Row 25: K2, sm, k6, *p1, k11; rep from * to last 9 sts, p1, k6, sm, k2.

Row 26: K2, sm, p6, *k1, p11; rep from * to last 9 sts, k1, p6, sm, k2.

Rows 3–26 set Triangle pattern.

Rep Rows 3–26 a further 5 times.

Next 2 rows: Knit, removing markers as you pass them.

Bind (cast) off knitwise.

Making Up and Finishing

Weave in loose ends and block to measurements.

tip

The stitch markers placed at each end act as a reminder to work the first and last two stitches in garter stitch for the border.

chapter 2 travel

fox cozy

Bring some wonderland charm to cooler days with this adorable
fox character cozy, complete with snuggly hood.

Materials
- Berroco Vintage light worsted (DK) weight yarn
  (52% acrylic/40% wool/8%nylon; 219yds/200m
  per 3½oz/100g ball)
  2 balls of shade 5176 Pumpkin (A)
  1 ball of shade 5105 Oats (B)
  1 ball of shade 5101 Mochi (C)
- US 10 (6mm) knitting needles
- Tapestry needle

Finished Measurements
13in (33cm) wide x 23in (59cm) long to top of hood

Gauge (Tension)
17 sts x 19 rows to measure 4in (10cm) over
stockinette (stocking) stitch on US 10 (6mm) needles
after blocking

Abbreviations
See page 127.

tips

Wind small balls of each yarn for working the intarsia sections so
you don't have to carry the yarn back and forth across the entire
width of the work.

Block out the sleep cozy and hood before affixing the ears and
stitching the features to make it easier to position them.

SAFETY NOTE: Do not leave babies to sleep unattended in a cozy.

For the Back
Using Yarn B and US 10 (6mm) needles, cast on 60 sts.
Rib rows 1–8: *K1, p1; rep from * to end.
Change to Yarn A and work in St st as follows:
Row 1 (RS): Knit.
Row 2 (WS): Purl.
Rows 3–60: Rep Rows 1–2 a further 29 times.
Change to Yarn B and work 6 rows in Rib as before.
Bind (cast) off in rib.

For the Front
Using Yarn B and US 10 (6mm) needles, cast on 60 sts.
Rib rows 1–8: *K1, p1; rep from * to end.
Change to Yarns A and C and work intarsia (see page
122) in St st as follows:
Note: The yarn color used is given after the number of
stitches to be worked. For example: K16A = knit 16
stitches in Yarn A.
Row 1 (RS): K16A, k28C, k16A.
Row 2 (WS): P16A, p28C, p16A.
Rows 3–48: Rep rows 1–2 a further 23 times.
Row 49: K18A, k24C, k18A.
Row 50: P18A, p24C, p18A.
Row 51: K20A, k20C, k20A.
Row 52: P20A, p20C, p20A.
Row 53: K22A, k16C, k22A.
Row 54: P22A, p16C, p22A.
Row 55: K24A, k12C, k24A.
Row 56: P24A, p12C, p24A.
Row 57: K25A, k10C, k25A.
Row 58: P26A, p8C, p26A.

Row 59: K27A, k6C, k27A.
Row 60: P28A, p4C, p28A.
Change to Yarn B and work 6 rows in Rib as before.
Bind (cast) off in rib.

For the Hood
Using Yarn B and US 10 (6mm) needles, cast on 60 sts.
Rib rows 1–6: *K1, p1; rep from * to end.
Change to Yarns A and C and work intarsia in
St st as follows:

Row 1 (RS): K15A, k13C, k4A, k13C, k15A.
Row 2 (WS): P15A, p12C, p6A, p12C, p15A.
Row 3: K15A, k11C, k8A, k11C, k15A.
Row 4: P16A, p10C, p8A, p10C, p16A.
Row 5: K16A, k9C, k10A, k9C, k16A.
Row 6: P17A, p8C, p10A, p8C, p17A.
Row 7: K17A, k7C, k12A, k7C, k17A.
Row 8: P18A, p6C, p12A, p6C, p18A.
Row 9: K18A, k5C, k14A, k5C, k18A.
Row 10: P19A, p4C, p14A, p4C, p19A.

Row 11: K19A, k3C, k15A, k3C, k19A.
Row 12: P20A, p2C, p15A, p2C, p20A.
Using Yarn A only, work St st for a further 27 rows.
Bind (cast) off.
Fold the bound (cast) off edge of the hood in half with WS together and join with mattress stitch (see page 124) to create the hood.
Using Yarn B and US 10 (6mm) needles, pick up and k48 sts along bottom edge just created, working across the seam.
Work 4 rows in Rib as before.
Bind (cast) off in Rib.

For the Outer Ears (make 2 alike)
Using Yarn A and US 10 (6mm) needles, cast on 14 sts.
Row 1 (RS): Knit.
Row 2 (WS): Purl.
Row 3: K2tog, k to last 2 sts, k2tog. (12 sts)
Row 4: Purl.
Row 5: K2tog, k to last 2 sts, k2tog. (10 sts)
Row 6: Purl.
Row 7: Knit.
Row 8: P2tog, p to last 2 sts, p2tog. (8 sts)
Row 9: Knit.
Row 10: Purl.
Row 11: K2tog, k to last 2 sts, k2tog. (6 sts)
Row 12: Purl.
Row 13: K2tog, k to last 2 sts, k2tog. (4 sts)
Row 14: Purl.
Bind (cast) off.

For the Inner Ears (make 2 alike)
Using Yarn C and US 10 (6mm) needles, cast on 14 sts.
Rows 1–2: Knit.
Row 3: K2tog, k to last 2 sts, k2tog. (12 sts)
Row 4: Knit.
Row 5: K2tog, k to last 2 sts, k2tog. (10 sts)
Rows 6–7: Knit.
Row 8: K2tog, k to last 2 sts, k2tog. (8 sts)

Rows 9–10: Knit.
Row 11: K2tog, k to last 2 sts, k2tog. (6 sts)
Row 12: Knit.
Row 13: K2tog, k to last 2 sts, k2tog. (4 sts)
Row 14: Knit.
Bind (cast) off.

Making Up and Finishing
Weave in all ends and block to measurements. Place the front and back pieces together and join the sides and base seam with mattress stitch. Position the hood in place along the upper ribbing on the back piece and join with mattress stitch.

Place the ears together in pairs of inner and outer ear pieces and join together. Stitch the ears securely in place and use some black yarn and satin stitch (see page 125) to embroider the eyes and nose to finish.

chevron stripes

In this bright geometric design, the repeating pattern of increases and decreases worked in playful stripes creates a striking chevron motif afghan.

Materials
- Mirasol Pima Kuri light worsted (DK) weight yarn (100% cotton; 208yds/190m per 3½oz/100g ball)
  1 ball of shade 14 Green (A)
  1 ball of shade 06 Midnight Pearl (B)
  1 ball of shade 03 Picket Fence (C)
  1 ball of shade 11 Darling Lilac (D)
  1 ball of shade 12 Raspberry Blush (E)
- US 6 (4mm) knitting needles
- Tapestry needle

Finished Measurements
22in (56cm) x 29½in (75cm)

Gauge (Tension)
20 sts x 25 rows to measure 4in (10cm) over chevron pattern on US 6 (4mm) needles after blocking

Abbreviations
See page 127.

For the Afghan
Using Yarn A and US 6 (4mm) needles, cast on 131 sts.
Row 1 (RS): *K1, yo, k4, k2tog, skpo, k4, yo; rep from * to last st, k1.
Row 2 (WS): Purl.
Rows 3–12: Rep Rows 1–2 a further 5 times.
Rows 13–24: Change to Yarn B and rep Rows 1–12.
Rows 25–36: Change to Yarn C and rep Rows 1–12.
Rows 37–48: Change to Yarn D and rep Rows 1–12.
Rows 49–60: Change to Yarn E and rep Rows 1–12.
Rep Rows 1–60 once more then Rows 1–59 only again.
(179 rows worked in total)
Bind (cast) off loosely purlwise.

Making Up and Finishing
Weave in all loose ends and block to measurements, taking care to pin out the chevron points at the top and bottom of the afghan.

tips
Creating stripes leaves a lot of yarn ends to weave in at the end of the work—try carrying them for a few stitches at the back of the work to make the finishing process easier.

make it yours

For a simpler but equally eye-catching finish, work the stripes in two contrasting shades of yarn.

lace receiving shawl

Ultra lightweight lace yarns are wonderful for keepsake baby gifts and this clever design, worked from the center out, with a pretty detailed border will be something to treasure for years to come. Additionally, the shawl multi-purposes as a coming home wrap, swaddling afghan, and cover-up when breastfeeding and is light enough to carry around in your baby essentials bag.

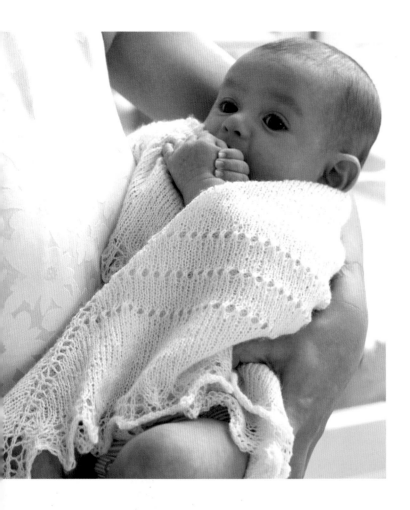

Materials
- Fyberspates Scrumptious Lace weight yarn (45% silk/55% wool; 1093yds/1000m per 3½oz/100g ball) 1 ball of shade 500 Natural
- US 3 (3.25mm) Double-pointed needles (DPNs) 8in (20cm) length—set of 5 needles
- US 3 (3.25mm) circular needles, 24in (60cm), 32in (80cm), and 40in (100cm) lengths
- 4 stitch markers
- Tapestry needle

Finished Measurements
27in (69cm) square

Gauge (Tension)
25 sts x 40 rows to measure 4in (10cm) over stockinette (stocking) stitch on US 3 (3.25mm) needles after blocking

Abbreviations
See page 127.

make it yours

Increase the size of the shawl by working
more rows of stockinette (stocking) stitch at
the center before commencing the border.
Ensure that the stitch count between corner
markers is a multiple of 8 stitches plus
3 before working the border.

For the Shawl

Using DPNs and leaving a 4in (10cm) tail, cast on 16 sts.

Row 1 (RS): Knit.

Row 2 (WS): Purl.

Join in the round and pm to indicate beginning of round.

Continue working in the round as follows, changing to circular needle as required:

Rounds 1–2 (RS): Knit.

Round 3: *K1, yo, k3, yo; rep from * a further 3 times. (24 sts)

Round 4: Knit.

Round 5: *K1, yo, k5, yo; rep from * a further 3 times. (32 sts)

Round 6: Knit.

Round 7: *K1, yo, k7, yo; rep from * a further 3 times. (40 sts)

Round 8: Knit.

Round 9: K1, yo, k9, yo, *pm, K1, yo, k9, yo; rep from * a further 2 times. (48 sts) (4 corner markers placed—beginning of round marker counts as 1 corner marker)

Round 10: Knit.

Continue in pattern as set, increasing 8 sts every other round for a further 60 rounds and changing needle

tips

Correcting mistakes when knitting lace can be very tricky. Try working in a lifeline—a piece of contrasting cotton run through the stitches every few rows. This will catch the stitches should you need to pull back any of the work.

Placing stitch markers at the four "spine" sections of the shawl will make it easy to identify where the increases need to be worked.

lengths as required. (288 sts)

Eyelet round: K1, yo, *[k2tog, yo] to 1 st before marker, k1, yo; rep from * to end of round.

Work 11 rounds in increase pattern as before. (336 sts)

Eyelet round: K1, yo, *[k2tog, yo] to 1 st before marker, k1, yo; rep from * to end of round.

Work 11 rounds in increase pattern as before. (384 sts)

Eyelet round: K1, yo, *[k2tog, yo] to 1 st before marker, k1, yo; rep from * to end of round.

Work 27 rounds in increase pattern as before. (496 sts)

For the Border

Eyelet round: *K1, yo, k2, [yo, k2, sl1, k2tog, psso, k2, yo, k1] to 1 st before marker, k1, yo; rep from * to end of round. (504 sts)

Next round: Knit.

Eyelet round: *K1, yo, k3, [yo, k2, sl1, k2tog, psso, k2, yo, k1] to 2 sts before marker, k2, yo; rep from * to end of round. (512 sts)

Next round: Knit.

Eyelet round: *K1, yo, k4, [yo, k2, sl1, k2tog, psso, k2, yo, k1] to 3 sts before marker, k3, yo; rep from * to end of round. (520 sts)

Next round: Knit.

Next round: K1, yo, k5, [yo, k7, yo, k1] to 4 sts before marker, k4, yo; rep from * to end of round.

Next round: Knit.

Bind (cast) off using the following elastic method: K1, backwards yo, k1, bring first st and yo over the k1 to bind (cast) off, continue to end.

Making Up and Finishing

Stitch up center hole to conceal using the yarn tail.
Weave in yarn ends and block firmly to measurements.

entrelac blanket

Build your skills with this impressive two-tone entrelac blanket. This design is created by working back and forth on each individual set of stitches, then picking up stitches to create the next set, resulting in an eye-catching woven effect.

Materials
- Rowan Pure Wool Worsted (aran) weight yarn (100% wool; 218yds/200m per 3½oz/100g ball)
  2 balls of shade 138 Azure (A)
  2 balls of shade 147 Breton (B)
- US 7 (4.5mm) knitting needles
- Tapestry needle

Finished Measurements
25in (64cm) x 23in (58cm)

Gauge (Tension)
20 sts and 25 rows to measure 4in (10cm) over stockinette (stocking) stitch on US 7 (4.5mm) needles after blocking

Abbreviations
See page 127.

For the Blanket
Using Yarn A and US 7 (4.5mm) needles, cast on 90 sts.

Foundation Triangles
The first triangle is worked over the first 6 cast-on sts with the remaining triangles worked on each following set of 6 cast-on sts.
Row 1 (WS): P2, turn the work.
Row 2 (RS): K2, turn the work.
Row 3: P3, turn.
Row 4: K3, turn.
Row 5: P4, turn.
Row 6: K4, turn.
Row 7: P5, turn.
Row 8: K5, turn.
Row 9: P6, **do not** turn.
Working over the next set of 6 sts along the cast-on edge in turn, work Rows 1–9 a further 14 times.
(15 foundation triangles)
Break Yarn A.

First Side Triangle
Join Yarn B.
Row 1 (RS): K2, turn the work.
Row 2 (WS): P2, turn the work.
Row 3: Kfb, ssk (working 1 Yarn B st and 1 Yarn A st), turn.
Row 4: P3, turn.
Row 5: Kfb, k1, ssk, turn.
Row 6: P4, turn.
Row 7: Kfb, k2, ssk, turn.
Row 8: P5, turn.
Row 9: Kfb, k3, ssk, **do not** turn.

Row 9: K5, ssk, turn.
Row 10: P6, turn.
Row 11: K5, ssk, turn.
Row 12: P6, turn.
Row 13: K5, ssk, **do not** turn. (1 rectangle made)
Rep Rows 1–13 to create rectangles across the row.

Second Side Triangle

Row 1 (RS): Pick up and k6 sts along edge of last block from row below, turn the work. (6 sts)
Row 2 (WS): P2tog, p4, turn the work. (5 sts)
Row 3: K5, turn.
Row 4: P2tog, p3, turn. (4 sts)
Row 5: K4, turn.
Row 6: P2tog, p2, turn. (3 sts)
Row 7: K3, turn.
Row 8: P2tog, p1, turn. (2 sts)
Row 9: K2, turn.
Row 10: P2tog, **do not** turn. (1 st)
Break Yarn B. First row complete.

Side Rectangle

Rejoin Yarn A.
Row 1 (WS): Pick up and p5 sts along edge of block from row below, turn the work. (6 sts on the needle)
Row 2 (RS): K6, turn the work.
Row 3: P5, p2tog (working 1 Yarn B st and 1 Yarn A st), turn.
Row 4: K6, turn.
Row 5: P5, p2tog, turn.
Row 6: K6, turn.
Row 7: P5, p2tog, turn.
Row 8: K6, turn.
Row 9: P5, p2tog, turn.
Row 10: K6, turn.
Row 11: P5, p2tog, turn.
Row 12: K6, turn.
Row 13: P5, p2tog, **do not** turn. (1 rectangle made)

First Rectangles

Row 1 (RS): Pick up and k6 sts along edge of block from row below, turn the work.
Row 2 (WS): P6, turn the work.
Row 3: K5, ssk (working 1 Yarn B st and 1 Yarn A st), turn.
Row 4: P6, turn.
Row 5: K5, ssk, turn.
Row 6: P6, turn.
Row 7: K5, ssk, turn.
Row 8: P6, turn.

Second Rectangles

Row 1 (WS): Pick up and p6 sts along edge of block from row below, turn the work.

Row 2 (RS): K6, turn the work.

Row 3: P5, p2tog (working 1 Yarn B st and 1 Yarn A st), turn.

Row 4: K6, turn.

Row 5: P5, p2tog, turn.

Row 6: K6, turn.

Row 7: P5, p2tog, turn.

Row 8: K6, turn.

Row 9: P5, p2tog, turn.

Row 10: K6, turn.

Row 11: P5, p2tog, turn.

Row 12: K6, turn.

Row 13: P5, p2tog, **do not** turn. (1 rectangle made)

Rep Rows 1–13 to create rectangles across the row. Break Yarn A. Second row complete.

Continue working the entrelac pattern, repeating the First Side Triangle, First Rectangles, Second Side Triangle, Side Rectangle, and Second Rectangles in the same order, alternating yarns, until work measures approx. 19in (64cm), ending after a Second Side Triangle.

Break Yarn B.

Bind (Cast) Off Triangles

Rejoin Yarn A.

Row 1 (WS): Pick up and p6 sts along edge of block from row below, turn the work. (7 sts on the needle)

Row 2 (RS): K7, turn.

Row 3: P2tog, p4, p2tog (working 1 Yarn B st and 1 Yarn A st), turn.

Row 4: K6, turn.

Row 5: P2tog, p3, p2tog, turn. (5 sts)

Row 6: K5, turn.

Row 7: P2tog, p2, p2tog, turn. (4 sts)

Row 8: K4, turn.

Row 9: P2tog, p1, p2tog, turn. (3 sts)

Row 10: K3, turn.

Row 11: P2tog, p2tog, turn. (2 sts)

Row 12: K2, turn.

Row 13: P3tog. (1 st)

Rep Rows 1–10 to create bound- (cast-) off triangles along the remainder of the row and fasten off.

For the Border

With RS facing, rejoin Yarn B at corner, pick up and k90 sts along one long edge. Knit 3 rows.

Bind (cast) off.

Rep for opposite long edge.

With RS facing, rejoin Yarn A at corner, pick up and k78 sts along one short edge.

Knit 3 rows.

Bind (cast) off.

Rep for opposite short edge.

Making Up and Finishing

Weave in all loose ends and block firmly to measurements.

tips

If you are taking a break whilst making this project, try to complete a full row of the design to help prevent you from losing your place in the pattern.

More confident knitters might prefer to knit backward as an alternative to purling, by working the knit stitch backward a purl stitch is created on the right side of the work and removes the need to continually turn the work and can speed up the make time.

make it yours

Chunky cables look great in bright bold color too—work with
a vibrant shade of yarn for a more dramatic finish.

cable blanket

There is nothing quite as cozy as a cable knit blanket. Worked in a traditional cream yarn, this version is given a modern twist with a brightly colored, simple crochet border.

Materials
- Rowan Brushed Fleece bulky (chunky) weight yarn (65% wool/30% alpaca/5% polymide; 115yds/105m per 1¾oz/50g ball) 3 balls of shade 251 Cove (A)
- Rowan Cotton Glace light worsted (DK) weight yarn (100% cotton; 126yds/115m per 1¾oz/50g ball) 1 ball of shade 856 Mineral (B)
- US 10½ (6.5mm) knitting needles
- US G/6 (4mm) crochet hook
- Cable needle
- Tapestry needle

Finished Measurements
18in (46cm) x 27in (69cm)

Gauge (Tension)
12 sts and 22 rows to measure 4in (10cm) over seed (moss) stitch on US 10½ (6.5mm) needles after blocking

Abbreviations
See page 127.

Cable Stitch
C6B: Slip 3 sts onto cable needle and hold at back of work, knit the next 3 sts on the knitting needle, knit the 3 sts from the cable needle (see page 121).

For the Blanket

Using Yarn A and US 10½ (6.5mm) needles, cast on 66 sts.

Row 1 (RS): *K1, p1; rep from * to end.

Row 2 (WS): *P1, k1; rep from * to end.

Rows 3–6: Rep Rows 1–2 twice more.

Work main pattern as follows:

Row 7: [K1, p1] 3 times, *p3, k6, p3, k2; rep from * twice more, p3, k6, p3, [k1, p1] 3 times.

Row 8: [P1, k1] 3 times, *k3, p6, k3, p2; rep from * twice more, k3, p6, k3, [p1, k1] 3 times.

Row 9: [K1, p1] 3 times, *p3, k6, p3, k2; rep from * twice more, p3, k6, p3, [k1, p1] 3 times.

Row 10: [P1, k1] 3 times, *k3, p6, k3, p2; rep from * twice more, k3, p6, k3, [p1, k1] 3 times.

Row 11: [K1, p1] 3 times, *p3, C6B, p3, k2; rep from * twice more, p3, C6B, p3, k2, [k1, p1] 3 times.

Row 12: [P1, k1] 3 times, *k3, p6, k3, p2; rep from * twice more, k3, p6, k3 [p1, k1] 3 times.

Rep Rows 7–12 until work measures 25½in (65cm) from cast-on edge ending with a WS row.

Next row (RS): *K1, p1; rep from * to end.

Next row (WS): *P1, k1; rep from * to end.

Rep last 2 rows twice more.

Bind (cast) off.

Making Up and Finishing

Weave in all loose ends and block to measurements.

For the Border

Note: US single crochet (sc) = UK double crochet (dc).

Using US G/6 (4mm) crochet hook, join Yarn B in a side stitch. Work 1ch then 1sc in each stitch around the blanket, working [1sc, 1ch, 1sc] in each corner. Join with a slip stitch in first stitch and fasten off. Weave in ends.

tips

Cables needles come in all shapes and sizes—be sure to select a large one to suit this chunky yarn.

Each row of the blanket is worked in different pattern sections combining seed (moss) stitch and cables. Help to keep track of each section by placing stitch markers between them.

hooded blanket

The perfect pre-bedtime snuggle blanket for baby. This super bulky wrap features a neat hood on one corner making it easy to keep little ones cozy and warm.

Materials

- Rowan Big Wool super bulky (super chunky) weight yarn (100% wool; 87yds/80m per 3½oz/100g ball)
  6 balls of shade 068 Sun
- US 15 (10mm) knitting needles
- Tapestry needle

Finished Measurements

30in (76cm) square

Gauge (Tension)

10 sts and 17 rows to measure 4in (10cm) over garter stitch on US 15 (10mm) needles after blocking

Abbreviations

See page 127.

make it yours

This straightforward design can be adapted to showcase fancy stitches, such as seed (moss) stitch or basket weave stitch, or work the hood and tassels in a contrast color for some two-tone fun.

For the Blanket

Using US 15 (10mm) needles,
cast on 75 sts.
Row 1: Knit.
Row 2: Knit.
Rows 1–2 set garter st.
Continue in garter st until work measures
30in (89cm) from cast-on edge.
Bind (cast) off.

For the Hood

Using US 15 (10mm) needles, cast on 3 sts.
Row 1 (RS): K1, kfb, k1. (4 sts)
Row 2 (WS): Purl.
Row 3: K1, kfb, kfb, k1. (6 sts)
Row 4: Purl.
Row 5: K1, kfb, k2, kfb, k1. (8 sts)
Row 6: Purl.
Row 7: K1, kfb, k to 2 sts from end, kfb, k1. (2 sts inc)
Row 8: Purl.
Rep Rows 7–8 until there are 48 sts on the needle,
ending with a purl row.
Bind (cast) off knitwise and leave a long tail to use for
seaming when breaking the yarn.

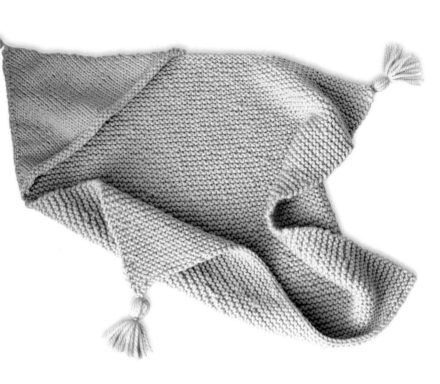

tips

Tassels should be firmly secured to ensure that they are not a hazard to small children. We suggest omitting these for very young babies.

When working the hood check the measurements against the blanket and work more rows to increase the size of the hood, or opt for fewer to make a smaller hood.

Making Up and Finishing

Weave in all loose ends and block to measurements.
Position the hood onto one corner of the blanket,
taking care to align the sides neatly. Use the long yarn
tail to oversew the pieces together. Fasten off and weave
in any remaining ends.

For the Tassels (make 3 alike)

Cut twelve 10in (25cm) lengths of yarn and leave two
of these lengths to one side. Fold the strands in half and
feed one of the remaining lengths through the upper
loop to create the hanging ties, knotting it securely
at the top of the bundle of yarn. With the final piece
of yarn, gather the tassel tightly approximately 1in
(2.5cm) from the folded top and wrap the remaining
piece of yarn in place and knot securely. Trim the ends
to neaten. Use the hanging ties to secure the tassels to
the top of the hood and each of the two side corners,
ensuring that they are stitched firmly in place.

cross motif blanket

Colorwork cross motifs create a bold and bright blanket with a modern graphic edge.

Materials
- Lion Brand Pound of Love worsted (aran) weight yarn (100% acrylic; 1019yds/932m per 15¾oz/448g ball)
  1 ball of shade 148 Turquoise (A)
  1 ball of shade 099 Antique White (B)
- US 10 (6mm) knitting needles
- 2 stitch markers
- Tapestry needle

Finished Measurements
19in (48.5cm) wide x 22in (56cm) long

Gauge (Tension)
20 sts x 22 rows to measure 4in (10cm) over stockinette (stocking) stitch on US 10 (6mm) needles after blocking

Abbreviations
See page 127.

make it yours

Reverse the placement of the yarns for this project to give the design a completely different finish, or play around with shades and work in stripes for a multicolored blanket.

For the Blanket

Using Yarn A and US 10 (6mm) needles, cast on 96 sts.

Rows 1–3: *K1, p1; rep from * to end.

Commence Cross Motif pattern

Work in St st changing color as indicated and carrying the unused yarn across the back.

Note: The yarn color used is given after the number of stitches to be worked. For example: K6A = knit 6 stitches in Yarn A.

Row 4 (WS): K3A, pm, using Yarn A only p to last 3 sts, pm, k3A.

Row 5 (RS): K3A, sm, using Yarn A only k to last 3 sts, sm, k3A.

Row 6: K3A, sm, using Yarn A only p to last 3 sts, pm, k3A.

Row 7: K3A, sm, *k6A, k6B, k6A; rep from * to marker, sm, k3A.

Row 8: K3A, sm, *p6A, p6B, p6A; rep from * to marker, sm, k3A.

Rows 9–12: Rep Rows 7–8.

Row 13: K3A, sm, *k1A, k16B, k1A; rep from * to

marker, sm, k3A.

Row 14: K3A, sm, *p1A, p16B, p1A; rep from * to marker, sm, k3A.

Rows 15–18: Rep Rows 13–14.

Rows 19–24: Rep Rows 7–8.

Row 25: K3A, sm, using Yarn A only k to last 3 sts, sm, k3A.

Rows 6–25 set Cross Motif pattern.

Rep Rows 6–25 a further 4 times.

Next row: K3A, sm, using Yarn A only p to last 3 sts, pm, k3A.

Next row: K3A, sm, using Yarn A only k to last 3 sts, pm, k3A.

Next 3 rows: Rep Rows 1–3, removing the markers as you pass them.

Bind (cast) off knitwise.

Making Up and Finishing

Weave in loose ends and block to measurements.

teddy travel blanket

skill rating
★★☆

Tote along this snug travel-sized blanket wherever you go! The blanket can be folded up and slid inside the custom pocket to make a sweet bear-faced pillow!

Materials

- Rowan Brushed Fleece super bulky (super chunky) weight yarn (65% wool/30% alpaca/5% polymide; 115yds/105m per 1¾oz/50g ball) 4 balls of shade 251 Cove (A)
- Rowan Alpaca Merino DK light worsted (DK) weight yarn (83% alpaca/7% wool/10% nylon; 115yds/105m per 1oz/25g ball) 4 balls of shade 104 Frisby (B)
- Small quantity of worsted (aran) weight yarn in black for features
- 2 buttons, 1in (2.5cm) diameter
- US 8 (5mm) knitting needles
- US 10½ (6.5mm) knitting needles
- Tapestry needle

Finished Measurements

Blanket: 23in (59cm) x 30in (76cm)

Gauge (Tension)

16 sts x 27 rows to measure 4in (10cm) over stockinette (stocking) stitch on US 8 (5mm) needles using Yarn B held double and after blocking

Abbreviations

See page 127.

For the Blanket

Using Yarn A and US 10½ (6.5mm) needles, cast on 80 sts.
Knit every row until blanket measures 30in (76cm).
Bind (cast) off.

For the Pocket Base

Holding two strands of Yarn B together, using US 8 (5mm) needles, cast on 50 sts.
Working with yarn held double throughout, continue as follows:
Row 1 (RS): Knit.
Row 2 (WS): Purl.
Rep Rows 1–2 until work measures 11in (28cm) from cast-on edge.
Next row (Rib): *K1, p1; rep from * to end.
Continue in Rib for 1in (2.5cm).
Bind (cast) off knitwise.

For the Bear Face

Using Yarn A and US 10½ (6.5mm) needles, cast on 15 sts.
Row 1: Knit.
Row 2: Kfb, k to last st, kfb. (17 sts)
Row 3: Knit.
Row 4: Kfb, k to last st, kfb. (19 sts)
Row 5: Knit.
Row 6: Kfb, k to last st, kfb. (21 sts)
Row 7: Knit.
Row 8: Kfb, k to last st, kfb. (23 sts)
Rows 9–12: Knit.
Row 13: K2tog, k to last 2 sts, k2tog. (21 sts)
Row 14: Knit.
Row 15: K2tog, k to last 2 sts, k2tog. (19 sts)
Row 16: Knit.
Row 17: K2tog, k to last 2 sts, k2tog. (17 sts)
Row 18: Knit.
Row 19: K2tog, k to last 2 sts, k2tog. (15 sts)
Bind (cast) off.

For the Ears (make 2 alike)

Holding two strands of Yarn B together, using US 8 (5mm) needles, cast on 13 sts.
Row 1 (RS): Knit.
Row 2 (WS): Purl.
Rows 3–12: Rep Rows 1–2.
Row 13: K2tog, k to last 2 sts, k2tog. (11 sts)
Row 14: Purl.
Row 15: K2tog, k to last 2 sts, k2tog. (9 sts)
Row 16: Purl.
Row 17: Kfb, k to last st, kfb. (11 sts)
Row 18: Purl.
Row 19: Kfb, k to last st, kfb. (13 sts)
Row 20: Purl.
Rows 21–30: Rep Rows 1–2.
Row 31: Purl.
Bind (cast) off.
Fold in half and join the two side seams with mattress stitch.

make it yours

Change up the colors and make
a koala, panda, or kitten
to add to the pocket.

Making Up and Finishing

Position the bear ears onto the upper portions of the pocket base (rib end) and pin in place.

With the black yarn embroider the nose of the bear onto the cream portion using the photographs as a reference, and pin into position to the front of the pocket base.

Once happy with the position of the face and ears sew securely into place. Sew buttons securely in place for eyes.

Place the embellished pocket wrong side up on one end of blanket, aligning the ribbed opening with the short edge of blanket and setting the pocket 7in (17.5cm) in from each side.

Sew along the sides and base with running stitch—leave the top (ribbed edge which is aligned with the top of blanket) unstitched.

Weave in all ends and block to neaten.

To make the blanket into a pillow

Fold the blanket into thirds with the pocket side facing downward, following the sides of the pocket as a guide. Fold the length of the blanket to cover the pocket on the reverse of the fold, insert hands into the pocket and turn inward so that the blanket is inside the pocket to create a pillow.

tips

Work neatly when securing the elements to the pocket as this will also be turned through so any visible stitches should be kept as neat as possible.

Take care when working with the yarns held double to ensure both strands are worked with each stitch, to avoid any unwanted loops or dropped stitches.

pixie baby nest

This pixie nest should fit perfectly in a baby stroller to keep little ones warm and cozy when out and about.

Materials
- Debbie Bliss Baby Cashmerino light worsted (DK) weight yarn (55% extrafine Merino wool/ 33% acrylic/12% cashmere; 136yds/125m per 1¾oz/50g ball) 4 balls of shade 065 Clotted Cream (A)
  1 ball of shade 067 Sienna (B)
- US 6 (4mm) knitting needles
- 3 buttons, ¾in (2cm) diameter
- Tapestry needle

Finished Measurements
11½in (29.5cm) wide x 22in (58cm) long to point of hood

Gauge (Tension)
21 sts x 34 rows to measure 4in (10cm) over garter stitch on US 6 (4mm) needles after blocking

Abbreviations
See page 127.

For the Baby Nest

For the Back and Hood

Using Yarn A and US 6 (4mm) needles, cast on 60 sts.
Knit every row until blanket measures 29in (73.5cm).
Bind (cast) off.

For the Right Side Panel

Using Yarn A and US 6 (4mm) needles, cast on 35 sts.
Knit 55 rows.
Bind (cast) off.

For the Left Side Panel

Using Yarn A and US 6 (4mm) needles, cast on 35 sts.
Knit 55 rows.
Next row (Buttonhole): *K7, yo, k2tog, k1; rep from * twice more, k to end.
Knit 3 rows.
Bind (cast) off.

make it yours

Increase the size of this baby nest by casting on more stitches and working more rows. Be sure to increase the sizing of the two front side panels and adjust the yarn amounts too.

Making Up and Finishing

Weave in all loose ends and gently block the panels.

Lay the back panel flat and fold the top two corners in to meet at the center. Using Yarn A and mattress stitch, join the seam to create the hood.

Fold the lower portion of the back piece up by 7in (17.5cm) to form the bottom part of the baby nest, and join side seams using Yarn A and mattress stitch. Place the two side panels on top of the back piece so that the lower edges of the panels lay along the top of the lower folded section and using Yarn A and mattress stitch (see page 124), join along the section where they meet the base. Using Yarn B and blanket stitch (see page 125), work along each side of the nest, joining the sides of the panels to the back piece.

Securely stitch the buttons in position.

Cut 18 lengths of Yarn B each 10in (25cm) long and set two aside. Fold the strands in half to make the tassel, feed one of the remaining lengths through the upper loop to create the hanging ties and knot securely at the top of the bundle of yarn. With the final piece of yarn, gather the tassel tightly 1in (2.5cm) from the folded top and wrap the remaining piece of yarn in place and knot securely.

Trim the ends to neaten. Stitch securely onto the top of the hood to finish.

chapter 3 play

patchwork toddler afghan

skill rating
★ ☆ ☆

Patchwork afghans are great fun to knit and the modular nature of the design means you can work with yarns from your stash and continue adding neat little squares to create an afghan as large as you like.

make it yours

Create a repeat pattern by working set numbers of squares in each color and laying them out in your chosen design before seaming.

Materials

- Cascade 220 and Cascade 220 Heathers* worsted (aran) weight yarn (100% Peruvian Highland wool; 220yds/200m per 3½oz/100g skein)

  1 skein of shade 9463B Gold (A)

  1 skein of shade 7814 Chartreuse (B)

  1 skein of shade 8010 Natural (C)

  1 skein of shade 8951 Aqua (D)

  1 skein of shade 7809 Violet (E)

  1 skein of shade 8863 Mellow Mauve (F)

  1 skein of shade 9420 Como Blue (G)

  1 skein of shade 9465B Burnt Orange (H)

  1 skein of shade 8906 Blue Topaz (I)

  1 skein of shade 8885 Dark Plum (J)

  1 skein of shade 9610 Azalea (K)

  1 skein of shade 7813 Jade (L)

  1 skein of shade 8836 Stonewash* (M)

  1 skein of shade 2451 Nectarine* (N)

  1 skein of shade 9605 Tiger Lily (O)

  1 skein of shade 7803 Magenta (P)
- US 8 (5mm) knitting needles
- Tapestry needle

Finished Measurements

28in (71cm) x 45in (115cm)

Gauge (Tension)

One seed (moss) stitch square (21 sts x 30 rows) to measure 5in (13cm) on US 8 (5mm) needles after blocking

Abbreviations

See page 127.

For the Individual Patchwork Squares

Using US 8 (5mm) needles, cast on 21 sts.

Rows 1–30: *K1, p1; rep from * to last st, k1.

Bind (cast) off leaving a long yarn tail.

Make a total of 60 Patchwork Squares in the following colors and quantities:

5 squares each in Yarns A, B, C, D, E, F, G, and H.

3 squares each in Yarns I, J, K, L, and M.

2 squares each in Yarns N and O.

1 square in P.

Making Up and Finishing

Block each of the Patchwork Squares to 5in (13cm) to achieve a neat and even finish. Arrange the squares into ten rows of six squares, arranging the colors until you are happy with the design. Join the squares using mattress stitch—working by joining the squares into pairs, then adding the pairs into rows. Once the rows are complete, join them together with mattress stitch to finish the afghan.

Weave in all loose ends and if necessary block the finished afghan to even all the seams out.

tips

Leave a long tail of yarn when casting on and binding (casting) off to use for seaming the squares together later.

If you are working with yarns from your stash, select yarns all of a similar weight, gauge (tension), and fiber as this will make the joining together much neater.

cotton backed afghan

The combination of this textured basket weave stitch and
the soft cotton backing gives this afghan a wonderfully cozy
finish and works well as a playmat for little ones.

Materials
- Lion Brand Vanna's Choice worsted (aran) weight yarn
  (100% acrylic; 170yds/156m per 3½oz/100g ball)
  4 balls of shade 099 Linen
- US 9 (5.5mm) knitting needles
- 2 stitch markers
- Tapestry needle
- 25¼ x 34½in (64 x 88cm) piece of printed cotton
  fabric
- Pins
- Sewing needle and matching thread

Finished Measurements
26in (66cm) x 36in (91cm)

Gauge (Tension)
16 sts x 25 rows to measure 4in (10cm) over Basket
Weave pattern on US 9 (5.5mm) needles after blocking

Abbreviations
See page 127.

tip
This pattern repeat is simple yet dramatic with no right or wrong side—
keeping a note of the row that you are on will help you to keep track
of your place in the pattern with ease.

For the Bottom Border
Using US 9 (5.5mm) needles, cast on 141 sts.
Rows 1–4: [K1, p1] to last st, k1.

For the Main Afghan
Note: You will continue to work the Border pattern
across 4 sts at each end of the row—two stitch markers
are placed on the next row (pm) as indicators that these
are the border sts. Slip the markers (sm) when you come
to them on subsequent rows.
Row 1: K1, p1, k1, p1, pm, k to last 4 sts, pm, p1, k1,
p1, k1.
Row 2: K1, p1, k1, p1, sm, p5, *k3, p5; rep from * to
last 4 sts, sm, p1, k1, p1, k1.
Row 3: K1, p1, k1, p1, sm, k5, *p3, k5; rep from * to
last 4 sts, sm, p1, k1, p1, k1.
Row 4: K1, p1, k1, p1, sm, k to last 4 sts, sm, p1, k1,
p1, k1.
Row 5: K1, p1, k1, p1, sm, k1, p3, *k5, p3; rep from *
to last 5 sts, k1, sm, p1, k1, p1, k1.
Row 6: K1, p1, k1, p1, sm, p1, k3, *p5, k3; rep from *
to last 5 sts, p1, sm, p1, k1, p1, k1.
Row 7: K1, p1, k1, p1, sm, k to last 4 sts, sm, p1, k1,
p1, k1.
Row 8: K1, p1, k1, p1, sm, p5, *k3, p5; rep from * to
last 4 sts, sm, p1, k1, p1, k1.
Row 9: K1, p1, k1, p1, sm, k5, *p3, k5; rep from * to
last 4 sts, sm, p1, k1, p1, k1.
Row 10: K1, p1, k1, p1, sm, k to last 4 sts, sm, p1, k1,
p1, k1.

make it yours

For an even cozier finish, switch the cotton lining material for a super-soft brushed flannel, but take care that baby does not overheat when wrapped up.

Row 11: K1, p1, k1, p1, sm, k1, p3, *k5, p3; rep from * to last 5 sts, k1, sm, p1, k1, p1, k1.

Row 12: K1, p1, k1, p1, sm, p1, k3, *p5, k3; rep from * to last 5 sts, p1, sm, p1, k1, p1, k1.

Rows 1–12 form the Basket Weave pattern.

Work repeats of Basket Weave pattern until work measures 25in (64cm) from cast-on edge ending with Row 10.

For the Top Border

Work Rows 1–4 as for Bottom Border. Bind (cast) off.

Making Up and Finishing

Weave in all loose ends and block to measurements. It is important to block the afghan before attaching the backing to ensure a smooth and neat finish. Press the fabric neatly and trim to ½in (1.5cm) larger than Basket Weave section of the afghan. Neatly fold the edges of the fabric ½in (1.5cm) in toward the wrong side and press in place. Pin to the back of the afghan, aligning the neat folded edges with the inside edges of the knitted border. With a sewing needle and coordinating cotton, secure the cotton to the afghan using neat slip stitches.

mitered squares blanket

Mitered squares are created by working decreases through the center
of the work to gradually bring in the sides and reveal a neat square.
These clever little blocks knit up surprisingly fast so before you know
it you have plenty for a lovely cozy blanket!

Materials

- Cascade 220 worsted (aran)
  weight yarn (100% Peruvian
  Highland wool; 220yds/200m per
  3½oz/100g skein)
  1 skein of shade 8509 Grey (A)
  1 skein of shade 7827 Goldenrod (B)
  1 skein of shade 9542 Blaze (C)
  1 skein of shade 8010 Natural (D)

1 skein of shade 8622 Camel (E)
1 skein of shade 8908 Anis (F)
- US 8 (5mm) knitting needles
- Stitch marker
- Tapestry needle

Finished Measurements
25in (64cm) square

Gauge (Tension)
1 mitered square to measure 4¾in
(12cm) square on US 8 (5mm)
needles

Abbreviations
See page 127.

For a Mitered Square

(make 36 in total; 6 in each color)
Using US 8 (5mm) needles and color of choice, cast on 36 sts placing a marker between sts 18 and 19 so there are 18 sts on each side of it.
Row 1: K to 2 sts before marker, ssk, sm, k2tog, k to end. (2 sts dec)
Row 2: Knit.
Rep Rows 1–2 until only 2 sts remain.
Next row: K2tog. (1 st)
Break yarn and pull through remaining st to fasten off.

Making Up and Finishing

Weave in all loose ends and block each square to measurements. Blocking the squares before seaming will make seaming much easier and ensure a neat finish. Lay the squares out following the chart.

1	E	D	B	F	C	A	1
2	F	C	A	E	D	B	2
3	E	D	B	F	C	A	3
4	F	C	A	E	D	B	4
5	E	D	B	F	C	A	5
6	F	C	A	E	D	B	6

make it yours

Mitered squares are great for using up yarn from your stash—work each square in a different shade or style of yarn for a really eclectic finish, remembering to work with yarns of a similar weight and gauge (tension) to ensure the squares join together neatly.

The orientation of the central diagonal decrease can be changed to create different finishes on the surface of the blanket.
Using mattress stitch, join the squares into pairs, then strips, and then join the strips.
Weave in any remaining ends and gently re-block to even out the seams.

tips

The stitch marker will ensure correct placement of the decreases down the center line.

To check the gauge (tension) of this pattern, make one mitered square using US 8 (5mm) needles. If it correctly measures 4¾in (12cm) square then continue using the US 8 (5mm) needles. If the square comes up smaller, switch to US 9 (5.5mm) needles and try again, whereas if the square comes up larger, switch to US 7 (4.5mm) needles and make a second square.

chunky openwork blanket

skill rating
★★☆

This lovely breathable fabric with pretty eyelet-hole details is worked in a chunky yarn for a fun modern twist. A larger gauge also makes this project a great starting point for those of you who are new to knitting lace patterns.

Materials
- Rowan Creative Focus Worsted (aran) weight yarn (75% wool/25% alpaca; 200yds/220m per 3½oz/100g ball)
  2 balls of shade 712 Lavender Heather
- US 10 (6mm) knitting needles
- Tapestry needle

Finished Measurements
22in (56cm) square

Gauge (Tension)
15 sts x 24 rows to measure 4in (10cm) over lace pattern on US 10 (6mm) needles after blocking

Abbreviations
See page 127.

Special Stitch
sl1, k2, psso: Slip 1 stitch knitwise, knit the next 2 stitches then pass the slipped stitched over the 2 stitches just knitted to decrease 1 stitch.

For the Blanket
Using US 10 (6mm) needles, cast on 88 sts.
Knit 3 rows.
Commence lace pattern:
Row 1 (RS): K4, *yo, sl1, k2, psso; rep from * to last 3 sts, k3.
Row 2 (WS): K2, p to last 2 sts, k2.
Row 3: K3, *yo, sl1, k2, psso; rep from * to last 4 sts, k4.
Row 4: K2, p to last 2 sts, k2.
Rep Rows 1–4 until work measures 18in (46cm) from cast-on edge.
Knit 2 rows.
Bind (cast) off knitwise.

Making Up and Finishing
Weave in all loose ends and block firmly to measurements to open up the lace stitches and reveal the detail of the blanket.

make it yours

For a brighter version work the blanket in a variegated yarn in rainbow shades or add a border in a contrasting color.

teddy comfort blanket

skill rating
★★☆

Add a cute little knitted character to the center
of this blanket to make a unique mini-comforter.

Materials

- Cascade 220 and Cascade 220 Heathers* worsted
  (aran) weight yarn (100% Peruvian Highland wool;
  220yds/200m per 3½oz/100g skein)
  1 skein of shade 9499 Sand (A)
  1 skein of shade 8622 Camel (B)
  1 skein of shade 9421 Blue Hawaii (C)
  1 skein of shade 2451 Nectarine* (D)
  Small quantity of 8555 Black (E)
- US 8 (5mm) knitting needles
- US 6 (4mm) double-pointed needles (DPNs), set of 5
- US H/8 (5mm) crochet hook
- Stitch marker
- Small quantity of toy stuffing
- Tapestry needle

Finished Measurements

20in (51cm) square

Gauge (Tension)

18 sts x 34 rows to measure 4in (10cm) over garter
stitch on US 8 (5mm) needles after blocking

Abbreviations

See page 127.

For the Blanket

Using Yarn A and US 8 (5mm) needles, cast on 60 sts.
Rows 1–100: Knit.
Bind (cast) off knitwise.

For the Borders

Using Yarn C and US 8 (5mm) needles, pick up and
k60 sts along the cast-on edge.
Rows 1–3: Knit.
Rows 4–8: Change to Yarn D and knit.
Row 9: K1, kfb, k to last 2 sts, kfb, k1. (62 sts)
Rows 10–11: Knit.
Row 12: K1, kfb, k to last 2 sts, kfb, k1. (64 sts)
Rows 13–17: Knit.
Row 18: K1, kfb, k to last 2 sts, kfb, k1. (66 sts)
Rows 19–20: Knit.
Row 21: K1, kfb, k to last 2 sts, kfb, k1. (68 sts)
Rows 22–24: Knit.
Bind (cast) off knitwise.
Rep to add identical border to the bound- (cast-) off
edge and then both row edges.

make it yours

Create your own custom design by adding a bunny or even a rag doll to the center of this comfort blanket.

For the Bear Head

Using Yarn A and US 6 (4mm) DPNs, cast on 20 sts. Divide equally over 4 needles (5 sts on each needle) and join for working in the round, placing a stitch marker to indicate beginning of round.

Round 1: Knit.
Round 2: *K1, kfb, k to last 2 sts on needle, kfb, k1; rep from * a further 3 times. (8 sts increased)
Rounds 3–10: Rep Rounds 1–2. (60 sts)
Rounds 11–13: Knit.
Break Yarn A and join Yarn B.
Rounds 14–19: Knit.
Round 20: *Ssk, k to last 2 sts on needle, k2tog; rep from * a further 3 times. (8 sts decreased)

tips

Be sure to use child-safe toy stuffing for the head of the bear. Fill it firmly and secure tightly to the blanket to avoid any hazards.

Use a stitch marker to indicate the beginning of the round when making the bear head.

Round 21: Knit.
Rounds 22–29: Rep Rounds 20–21. (20 sts)
Round 30: Rep Round 20. (12 sts)
Stuff head with toy stuffing until firm, then break yarn leaving a long tail and draw through all stitches, pulling firmly to close the hole and secure inside of the head.

For the Ears (make 2 alike)

Using Yarn B and US6 (4mm) DPNs, cast on 8 sts. Divide equally over 4 needles (2 sts on each needle) and join for working in the round, placing a stitch marker to indicate beginning of round.

Round 1: Knit.
Round 2: Kfb in each st. (16 sts)
Round 3: Knit.
Round 4: *K1, [kfb] twice, k1; rep from * a further 3 times. (24 sts)
Rounds 5–7: Knit.
Bind (cast) off using the 3-needle bind (cast) off method.

For the Crochet Border

Note: US single crochet (sc) = UK double crochet (dc). Using Yarn A and US H/8 (5mm) crochet hook, join yarn anywhere along one side edge and work 1ch, then 1sc in each row end and stitch around working [1sc, 1ch, 1sc] in each corner.

Making Up and Finishing

Sew ears in place on top of bear head and use Yarn E to embroider eyes, nose, and mouth. Sew bear head securely in place in center of blanket.
Weave in all loose ends and block to measurements.

mountain motif blanket

Make playtime more fun with this mountain range scene—
perfect to inspire budding adventurers. Worked in super soft
worsted (aran) weight yarns, this is ideal for snuggling.

Materials
- Brown Sheep Company Lamb's Pride worsted (aran)
  weight yarn (85% wool/15% mohair; 190yds/173m
  per 4oz/113g ball)
  1 ball of shade M187 Turquoise Depths (A)
  1 ball of shade M16 Seafoam (B)
  1 ball of shade M82 Blue Flannel (C)
  1 ball of shade M59 Periwinkle (D)
  1 ball of shade M10 Creme (E)
- US 8 (5mm) knitting needles
- 2 stitch makers
- Tapestry needle

Finished Measurements
18in (46cm) x 20½in (52.5cm)

Gauge (Tension)
17 sts x 24 rows to measure 4in (10cm) over
stockinette (stocking) stitch on US 8 (5mm) needles
after blocking

Abbreviations
See page 127.

For the Blanket
Using Yarn A and US 8 (5mm) needles, cast on 75 sts.
Rows 1–5: Knit.
Row 6 (RS): K5, pm, k to last 5 sts, pm, k5.
Row 7 (WS): K5, sm, p to next marker, sm, k5.
Row 8: K5, sm, k to next marker, sm, k5.
Rows 9–14: Rep Rows 7–8.
Row 15: Rep Row 7.
Work Chart (see page 93) as follows:
Row 1 (RS): K5, sm, working in st st and using the
stranded colorwork technique, work Row 1 of Chart to
next marker, sm, k5.
Row 2 (WS): K5, sm, working in st st and using the
stranded colorwork technique, work Row 2 of Chart to
next marker, sm, k5.
Maintaining garter st borders as set and working the
next row of the Chart between the markers, continue
in St st and using the stranded or intarsia colorwork
techniques as appropriate, continue as set to end of
Row 90.
Continue in Yarn D, only slipping the markers as you
pass them.
Next row (RS): Knit.
Next row (WS): K5, sm, p to next marker, k5.
Rep last 2 rows a further 3 times.
Next 5 rows: Knit.
Bind (cast) off.

Making Up and Finishing
Weave in all loose ends and block to measurements.

mountain
motif chart

KEY

▢ Turquoise Depths (A)
▢ Seafoam (B)
■ Blue Flannel (C)
▢ Periwinkle (D)
▢ Creme (E)

tips

To help prevent getting in a tangle when working with multiple yarn colors, place each individual ball in a yarn bowl or zip-lock bag.

Combine your skills, switching between the stranded colorwork and intarsia techniques where appropriate—use the stranded technique for the lower rows where you change color more than twice and intarsia for larger blocks of color in the higher mountains and sky.

make it yours

If you want to add additional embellishments to the scene, why not duplicate stitch some flowers to the foreground or add a few clouds to the sky after finishing and blocking the main knitted blanket.

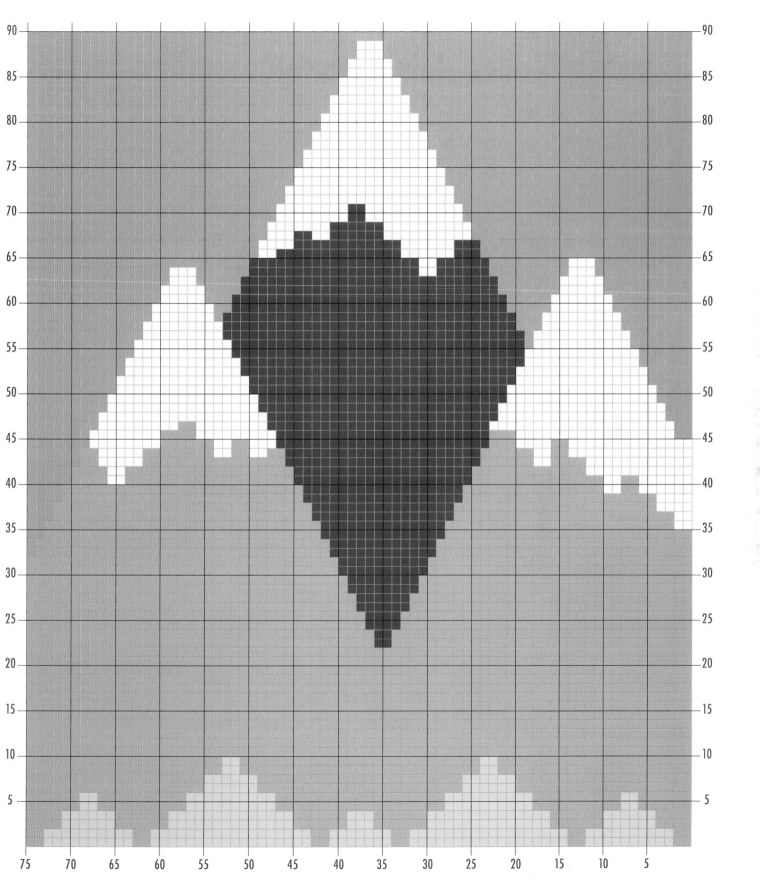

popcorn stitch blanket

This tactile blanket is cozy and colorful. The textured surface of the popcorn stitch is not only fun to knit but will look super-cute in a play room or on a stroller.

Materials
- Lion Brand Vanna's Choice worsted (aran) weight yarn (100% acrylic; 170yds/156m per 3½oz/100g ball)
  2 balls of shade 102 Aqua (A)
  1 ball of shade 100 White (B)
- US 10 (6mm) knitting needles
- Tapestry needle

Finished Measurements
20½in (52cm) wide x 22in (58cm)

Gauge (Tension)
20 sts x 18 rows to measure 4in (10cm) over popcorn stitch on US 10 (6mm) needles after blocking

Abbreviations
See page 127.

tip
The popcorn stitch is created by working a k3tog to decrease 2 stitches and a [k1, p1, k1] into one stitch to increase 2 stitches. By working these two stitches together in the same row they will balance each other out and the stitch count will remain constant.

For the Blanket
Using Yarn A and US 10 (6mm) needles, cast on 66 sts.
Rows 1–2: Knit.
Row 3 (WS): Knit.
Row 4 (RS): K1, *[k1, p1, k1] into next st, k3tog; rep from * to last st, k1.
Row 5: Knit.
Row 6: K1, *k3tog, [k1, p1, k1] into next st; rep from * to last st, k1.
Rep Rows 3–6 until work measures 17in (43cm) ending with Row 6.
Next 2 rows: Knit.
Bind (cast) off knitwise.

For the Border
With RS facing, using Yarn B and US 10 (6mm) needles, pick up and k68 sts along one row-edge side of the blanket.
Knit 8 rows.
Bind (cast) off knitwise.
Rep for the opposite row-edge side.
With RS facing, using Yarn B and US 10 (6mm) needles, join yarn at corner of piece and pick up and k75 sts along bottom (bound-/cast-on) edge of the blanket (including along edge of the border just worked).
Knit 8 rows.
Bind (cast) off knitwise.
Rep for the opposite top (bound-/cast-off) edge.

make it yours

For a simpler look, work the border and blanket in the same colors or work stripes changing color every four rows.

With RS facing, using Yarn A and US 10 (6mm) needles, join yarn at corner of piece and pick up and k75 sts along the side edge of blanket (including along edge of the border just worked).
Knit 15 rows.
Bind (cast) off knitwise.
Rep for opposite side edge.
With RS facing, using Yarn A and US 10 (6mm) needles, join yarn at corner of piece and pick up and

k89 sts along bottom edge of the blanket (including along edge of the border just worked).
Knit 11 rows.
Bind (cast) off knitwise.
Rep for top edge.

Making Up and Finishing

Weave in all loose ends and block to measurements.

skinny stripes

This classic striped design is simple and easy to make and by working with two shades of one color you can easily create a subtle ombré effect.

Materials
- Lion Brand Pound of Love worsted (aran) weight yarn (100% acrylic; 1019yds/932m per 15¾oz/448g ball)
  1 ball of shade 099 Antique White (A)
  1 ball of shade 148 Turquoise (B)
  1 ball of shade 106 Pastel Blue (C)
- US 10 (6mm) knitting needles
- Tapestry needle

Finished Measurements
26¾in (56cm) x 28¼in (72cm)

Gauge (Tension)
16 sts x 28 rows to measure 4in (10cm) over garter stitch on US 10 (6mm) needles after blocking

Abbreviations
See page 127.

make it yours

Create a candy-striped effect by working with alternate rows of the contrast colors.

For the Blanket

Using Yarn A and US 10 (6mm) needles, cast on 100 sts.

Rows 1–5: Knit.

Rows 6–7: Change to Yarn B. Knit.

Rows 8–9: Change to Yarn A. Knit.

Rows 10–73: Rep Rows 6–9.

Rows 74–75: Change to Yarn C. Knit.

Rows 76–77: Change to Yarn A. Knit.

Rows 78–141: Rep Rows 74–77.

Rows 142–143: Change to Yarn B. Knit.

Rows 144–145: Change to Yarn A. Knit.

Rows 146–209: Rep Rows 142–145.

Rows 210–211: Using Yarn A, knit.

Bind (cast) off knitwise.

For the Border

With RS facing, using Yarn A and US 10 (6mm) needles, pick up and k108 sts along the side edge.

Knit 4 rows.

Bind (cast) off knitwise.

Rep to add a second identical border on opposite side.

Making Up and Finishing

Weave in all loose ends and block to measurements.

tip

Carrying the yarns at the side of the work will reduce the number of times the yarn is cut and therefore the number of ends to weave in.

bobble blanket

Add a splash of fun to the nursery with this sweet blanket, knitted with multi-colored, tactile bobbles.

Materials
- Lion Brand Modern Baby light worsted (DK) weight yarn (50% acrylic/50% nylon; 173yds/158m per 2½oz/75g ball)
  2 balls of shade 098 Cream (A)
  1 ball of shade 147 Purple (B)
  1 ball of shade 102 Pink (C)
  1 ball of shade 194 Chartreuse (D)
  1 ball of shade 133 Orange (E)
  1 ball of shade 148 Turquoise (F)
- US 7 (4.5mm) knitting needles
- US G/6 (4mm) crochet hook
- Tapestry needle

Finished Measurements
17½in (44cm) wide x 24in (61cm) long

Gauge (Tension)
17 sts x 29 rows to measure 4in (10cm) over stockinette (stocking stitch) on US 7 (4.5mm) needles after blocking

Abbreviations
See page 127.

Special Stitch
MB (Make Bobble): Knit into the front then back, front then back, and front again of the next stitch, turn and purl these 5 stitches, turn and knit these 5 stitches, turn and purl these 5 stitches, turn and knit these 5 stitches, * pass the second stitch on the right-hand needle over the first stitch and off needle, rep from * 3 more times (1 stitch remains).

For the Blanket
Using Yarn A and US 7 (4.5mm) needles, cast on 77 sts.
Row 1 (RS): Knit.
Row 2 (WS): Purl.
Rows 3–10: Rep Rows 1–2.
Row 11 (Bobbles): K5, *using Yarn B, MB, using Yarn A, k5; rep from * to end.
Row 12: Purl.
Rows 13–20: Rep Rows 1–2.
Rows 11–20 set Bobble pattern.
Continue working reps of Rows 11–20 changing the color of the bobbles in each bobble row in the following order: Yarn C, Yarn D, Yarn E, Yarn F.
Rep this five-color sequence 3 times in total, ending on Row 20. (160 rows worked in total)
Bind (cast) off knitwise.

Making Up and Finishing
Weave in loose ends and block to measurements.

For the Border
Note: US single crochet (sc) = UK double crochet (dc).
Using US G/6 (4mm) crochet hook, join Yarn D in any stitch along one side. ** Work 1ch (does not count as st), then 1sc in each st and row end around working [1sc, 1ch, 1sc], join with sl st in first st. Rep from ** once more to create a second round, working 1sc in each st around and [1sc, 1ch, 1sc] in each corner ch-sp. Fasten off and weave in remaining ends.

make it yours

This blanket is worked with a selection of
rainbow colored bobbles, alternatively the
main section of the blanket could be knit
in a favorite color and the bobbles worked
in cream yarn.

chevron eyelet lace

skill rating
★★☆

This repeated pattern of simple eyelets creates a neat chevron pattern which, when worked in a bold variegated yarn, produces a modern lace design.

Materials
- Brown Sheep Company Lamb's Pride worsted (aran) weight yarn (85% wool/15% mohair; 190yds/173m per 4oz/113g ball)
  3 balls of shade M200 Strawberry Smoothie
- US 8 (5mm) knitting needles
- 2 stitch markers
- Tapestry needle

Finished Measurements
26½in (67.5cm) wide x 30in (76cm) long

Gauge (Tension)
17 sts x 24 rows to measure 4in (10cm) over lace pattern on US 8 (5mm) needles after blocking

Abbreviations
See page 127.

For the Blanket
Using US 8 (5mm) needles, cast on 107 sts.
Row 1: K4, pm, k to last 4 sts, pm, k4.
Rows 2–4: K4, sm, k to marker, sm, k4.

tip
The stitch markers placed at each end act as a reminder to work the first and last four stitches in garter stitch for the border.

Row 5 (RS): K4, sm, k1, *k5, yo, k2tog, k1; rep from * to last 6 sts, k2, sm, k4.
Row 6 (WS): K4, sm, p to marker, sm, k4.
Row 7: K4, sm, k1, *k3, ssk, yo, k1, yo, k2tog; rep from * to last 6 sts, k2, sm, k4.
Row 8: K4, sm, p to marker, sm, k4.
Row 9: K4, sm, k2, *k1, ssk, yo, k3, yo, k2tog; rep from * to last 5 sts, k1, sm, k4.
Row 10: K4, sm, p to marker, sm, k4.
Row 11: K4, sm, k1, *yo, ssk, k1, pass second st on right needle over first st and off the needle, yo, k5; rep from * to last 6 sts, k2, sm, k4.
Row 12: K4, sm, p to marker, sm, k4.
Row 13: K4, sm, k1, *k1, kfb, k6; rep from * to last 6 sts, k2, sm, k4.
Row 14: K4, sm, p to marker, sm, k4.
Row 15: K4, sm, k1, *k2tog, k4, yo, k2tog, k1; rep from * to last 6 sts, k2, sm, k4.
Row 16: K4, sm, p to marker, sm, k4.
Rows 5–16 set Chevron pattern.
Rep Rows 5–16 a further 14 times.
Next 3 rows: Knit, removing markers as you pass them.
Bind (cast) off knitwise.

Making Up and Finishing
Weave in all loose ends and block firmly to measurements to open up the lace pattern.

make it yours

For a more classic style, work this blanket in a solid light pastel shade of yarn.

colorwork triangles

The bright, bold triangles set-off against a neutral background will appeal to all young children. This design is surprisingly simple to follow and makes a great project for knitters who are new to the technique.

Materials

- Brown Sheep Company Lamb's Pride worsted (aran) weight yarn (85% wool/15% mohair; 190yds/173m per 4oz/113g ball)
  2 balls of shade M10 Creme (A)
  1 ball of shade M22 Autumn Harvest (B)
  1 ball of shade M59 Periwinkle (C)
  1 ball of shade M14 Sunburst Gold (D)
  1 ball of shade M65 Sapphire (E)
- US 8 (5mm) knitting needles
- 2 stitch markers
- Tapestry needle

Finished Measurements

22½in (56cm) x 24in (62cm)

Gauge (Tension)

17 sts x 24 rows to measure 4in (10cm) over stockinette (stocking) stitch on US 8 (5mm) needles

Abbreviations

See page 127.

make it yours

Supersize this design by casting on more stitches to work more triangles per row and continue to add in more pattern repeats to make it larger. Remember to adjust yarn quantities accordingly.

colorwork triangles chart

KEY

☐ Cream (A)   ■ Periwinkle (C)   ■ Sapphire (E)
▦ Autumn Harvest (B)   ▦ Sunburst Gold (D)

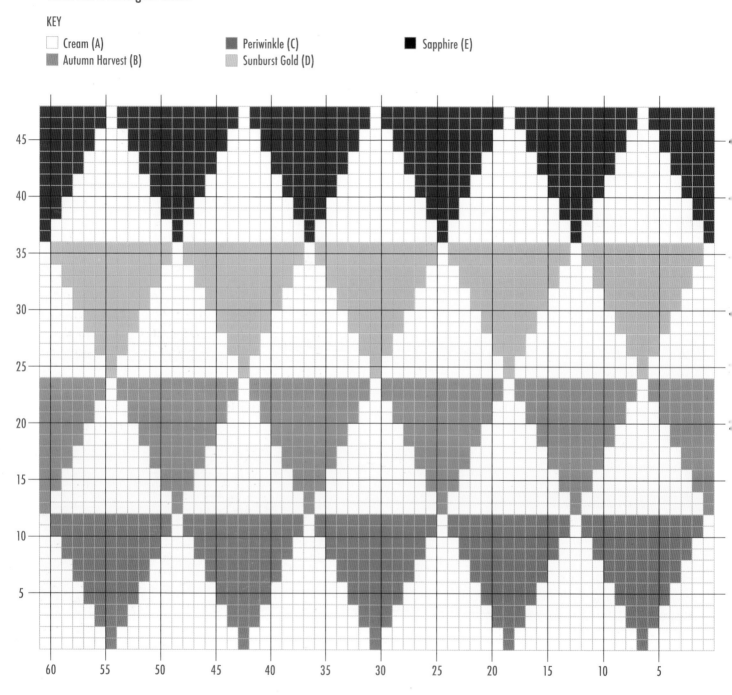

tips

To help prevent getting in a tangle when working with multiple yarn colors, place each individual ball in a yarn bowl or zip-lock bag.

For the Blanket

Using Yarn A and US 8 (5mm) needles, cast on 67 sts. Knit 3 rows.

Working in St st between markers, keeping 3 edge sts on each side in garter st and using the stranded colorwork technique throughout, commence Chart as follows:

Row 1 (RS): K3, pm, work Row 1 of Chart, pm, k3.
Row 2 (WS): K3, sm, work Row 2 of Chart, sm, k3.
Continue to work through Chart until two full repeats of the 48-row pattern have been worked (96 chart rows in total).
Using Yarn A, knit 3 rows.
Bind (cast) off knitwise.

For the Border

With RS facing, using Yarn A and US 8 (5mm) needles, pick up and k53 sts along one long side.
Rows 1–4: Knit.
Rows 5–6: Change to Yarn B. Knit.
Rows 7–8: Change to Yarn A. Knit.
Rows 9–10: Change to Yarn C. Knit.
Rows 11–12: Change to Yarn A. Knit.
Rows 13–14: Change to Yarn D. Knit.
Rows 15–16: Change to Yarn A. Knit.
Rows 17–18: Change to Yarn E. Knit.

Rows 19–21: Change to Yarn A. Knit.
Bind (cast) off knitwise.
Rep to add a second identical border on opposite side.
With RS facing, using Yarn A and US 8 (5mm) needles, pick up and k98 sts along row edge of border, cast-on edge of center piece and row edge of opposite border.
Rep Rows 1–21 of Border sequence then add a second identical border to bound- (cast-) off edge in the same manner.

Making Up and Finishing

Weave in all loose ends and block to measurements.

rainbow blanket

This brightly striped blanket is a great gift for little boys and girls alike and each color change is marked by simple eyelets created with a very basic lace stitch to add a charming detail to this quick-make design.

Materials

- Rowan Baby Merino Silk DK light worsted (DK) weight yarn (66% wool/34% silk; 148yds/135m per 1¾oz/50g ball)

  1 ball of shade 687 Strawberry (A)

  1 ball of shade 688 Sunshine (B)

  1 ball of shade 678 Rose (C)

  1 ball of shade 677 Teal (D)

  1 ball of shade 701 Aubergine (E)

  1 ball of shade 686 Cantaloupe (F)

  1 ball of shade 697 Grasshopper (G)
- US 6 (4mm) knitting needles
- Tapestry needle

Finished Measurements

19in (48cm) x 28in (71cm)

Gauge (Tension)

21 sts and 40 rows to measure 4in (10cm) over garter stitch on US 6 (4mm) needles after blocking

Abbreviations

See page 127.

For the Blanket

Using Yarn A and US 6 (4mm) needles, cast on 100 sts.

Rows 1–20: Knit.

Break Yarn A and change to Yarn B.

Row 21 (Eyelet row): K2, *k2tog, yo; rep from * to last 2 sts, k2.

Rows 22–40: Knit.

Break Yarn B, change to Yarn C and rep Rows 21–40.

Break Yarn C, change to Yarn D and rep Rows 21–40.

Break Yarn D, change to Yarn E and rep Rows 21–40.

Break Yarn E, change to Yarn F and rep Rows 21–40.

Break Yarn F, change to Yarn G and rep Rows 21–40.

Break Yarn G, change to Yarn A and rep Rows 21–40.

Break Yarn A, change to Yarn B and rep Rows 21–40.

Continue working in stripes as established until you have completed two full sets of seven-color stripes. Bind (cast) off.

Making Up and Finishing

Weave in all loose ends and block to measurements.

make it yours

Create an ombré design by working with a selection of tonal shades of the same color yarn.

tips

Striped designs can leave lots of yarn ends to weave in when finishing—try holding the yarn tail against the work and catching it as you work the stitches to weave in the yarn as a new color is added.

Using a row counter is a great way to keep track of the rows worked between color changes and if you get lost try counting the garter stitch ridges—each ridge equals two rows.

navajo motif blanket

skill rating
★★★

Add a colorful flash to a stroller with this bold knitted blanket.
The stranded colorwork motif is knit in bright shades for big
impact and the blanket is accentuated with a deep crochet border.

Materials
- Brown Sheep Company Lamb's Pride worsted (aran)
  weight yarn (85% wool/15% mohair; 190yds/173m
  per 4oz/113g ball)
  2 balls of shade M01 Sandy Heather (A)
  1 ball of shade M82 Blue Flannel (B)
  1 ball of shade M14 Sunburst Gold (C)
  1 ball of shade M187 Turquoise Depths (D)
  1 ball of shade M159 Deep Coral (E)
- US 8 (5mm) knitting needles
- US H/8 (5mm) crochet hook
- Tapestry needle

Finished Measurements
21½in (55cm) x 27½in (70cm)

Gauge (Tension)
17 sts x 24 rows to measure 4in (10cm) over
stockinette (stocking stitch) on US 8 (5mm) needles
after blocking

Abbreviations
See page 127.

make it yours

For a more subtle finish, work with a selection of different shades of
the same color to team with the neutral background.

For the Blanket

Using Yarn A and US 8 (5mm) needles, cast on 66 sts.

Row 1 (WS): K3, pm, k to last 3 sts, pm, k3.

Rows 2–3: K3, sm, k to marker, sm, k3.

Row 4: K3, sm, k to marker, sm, k3.

Row 5: K3, sm, p to marker, sm, k3

Rows 6–11: Rep Rows 4–5.

Begin working from Chart as follows:

Row 1 (RS): K3, sm, using the stranded colorwork technique when necessary and working in St st, work Row 1 of Chart to next marker, sm, k3.

Row 2 (WS): K3, sm, using the stranded colorwork technique when necessary and working in St st work Row 2 of Chart to next marker, sm, k3.

Maintaining garter st borders as set and working the next row of the Chart between the markers, continue as set to end of Row 54, then work the Chart in reverse (see Tips box) once more. (110 Chart rows worked)

Row 1: K3, sm, k to marker, sm, k3.

Row 2: K3, sm, p to marker, sm, k3.

Rows 3–8: Rep Rows 4–5.

Rows 9–11: K3, sm, k to marker, sm, k3.

Bind (cast) off knitwise.

For the Crochet Border

Note: US single crochet (sc) = UK double crochet (dc).

Round 1: Using Yarn C and US H/8 (5mm) crochet hook, join yarn in one side edge and work 1ch, then 1sc in each row end and stitch around working [1sc, 1ch, 1sc] in each corner, join with sl st in first sc.

Continue working repeats of Round 1 using the following colors:

Round 2: Yarn C.

Round 3: Yarn B.

Rounds 4–5: Yarn E.

Rounds 6–7: Yarn D.

Rounds 8–11: Yarn A.

Rounds 12–13: Yarn C.

Round 14: Yarn B.

Fasten off.

Making Up and Finishing

Weave in all loose ends and block to measurements.

tips

The chart is read from bottom to top and from right to left on RS (odd) rows, and left to right on WS (even) rows. After completing the chart once you will need to work a mirror image; do this by turning the chart so that the top row becomes the bottom row.

When carrying the yarn at the back of the work, keep the floats smaller than usual, catching them every couple of stitches to prevent small fingers from becoming caught in them.

make it yours

To make a sweet comforter, simply omit the crochet
border, finishing the edge with blanket stitch instead.

navajo motif chart

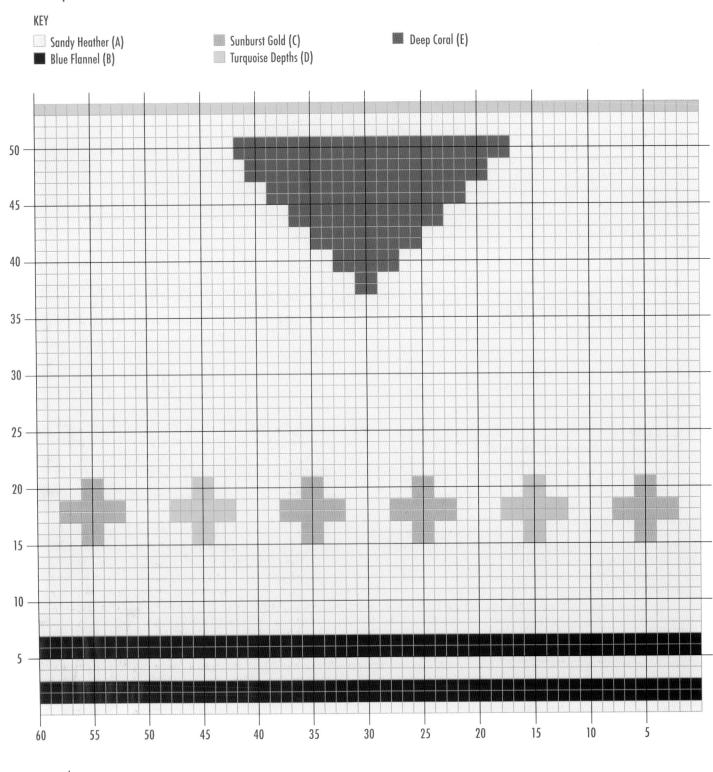

techniques

Gauge (tension)

A gauge (tension) is given with each pattern to help you make your item the same size as the sample. The gauge (tension) is given as the number of stitches and rows you need to work to produce a 4in (10cm) square of knitting.

Using the recommended yarn and needles, cast on 8 stitches more than the gauge (tension) instruction asks for—so if you need to have 10 stitches to 4in (10cm), cast on 18 stitches. Working in pattern as instructed, work eight rows more than is needed. Bind (cast) off loosely.

Lay the swatch flat without stretching it. Lay a ruler across the stitches as shown, with the 2in (5cm) mark centered on the knitting, then put a pin in the knitting at the start of the ruler and at the 4in (10cm) mark: the pins should be well away from the edges of the swatch. Count the number of stitches between the pins. Repeat the process across the rows to count the number of rows to 4in (10cm).

If the number of stitches and rows you've counted is the same as the number asked for in the instructions, you have the correct gauge (tension). If you do not have the same number then you will need to change your gauge (tension).

To change gauge (tension) you need to change the size of your knitting needles. A good rule of thumb to follow is that one difference in needle size will create a difference of one stitch in the gauge (tension). You will need to use larger needles to achieve fewer stitches and smaller ones to achieve more stitches.

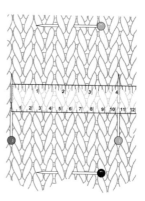

Holding needles

If you are a knitting novice, you will need to discover which is the most comfortable way for you to hold your needles.

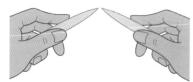

Like a knife

Pick up the needles, one in each hand, as if you were holding a knife and fork—that is to say, with your hands lightly over the top of each needle. As you knit, you will tuck the blunt end of the right-hand needle under your arm, let go with your hand and use your hand to manipulate the yarn, returning your hand to the needle to move the stitches along.

Like a pen

Now try changing the right hand so you are holding the needle as you would hold a pen, with your thumb and forefinger lightly gripping the needle close to its pointed tip and the shaft resting in the crook of your thumb. As you knit, you will not need to let go of the needle but simply slide your right hand forward to manipulate the yarn.

Holding yarn

As you knit, you will be working stitches off the left needle and onto the right needle, and the yarn you are working with needs to be tensioned and manipulated to produce an even fabric. To hold and tension the yarn you can use either your right or left hand, depending on the method you are going to use to make the stitches.

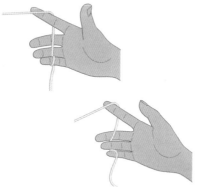

Yarn in right hand

To knit and purl in the US/UK style (see page 117), hold the yarn in your right hand. You can wind the yarn around your fingers in different ways, depending on how tightly you need to hold it to achieve an even gauge (tension). Try both ways shown to find out which works best for you.

To hold the yarn tightly (above, top), wind it right around your little finger, under your ring and middle fingers, then pass it over your index finger, which will manipulate the yarn.

For a looser hold (above), catch the yarn between your little and ring fingers, pass it under your middle finger, then over your index finger.

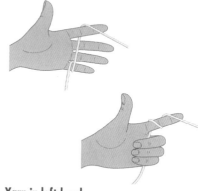

Yarn in left hand

To knit and purl in the continental style (see page 117–118), hold the yarn in your left hand. This method is sometimes easier for left-handed people to use, though many left-handers are quite comfortable knitting with the yarn in their right hand. Try the ways shown to find out which works best for you.

To hold the yarn tightly (above, top), wind it right around your little finger, under your ring and middle fingers, then pass it over your index finger, which will manipulate the yarn.

For a looser hold (above), fold your little, ring, and middle fingers over the yarn, and wind it twice around your index finger.

Making a slip knot

You will need to make a slip knot to form your first cast-on stitch.

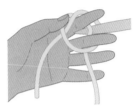 

1 With the ball of yarn on your right, lay the end of the yarn on the palm of your left hand and hold it in place with your left thumb. With your right hand, take the yarn around your top two fingers to form a loop. Take the knitting needle through the back of the loop from right to left and use it to pick up the strand nearest to the yarn ball, as shown in the diagram. Pull the strand through to form a loop at the front.

2 Slip the yarn off your fingers, leaving the loop on the needle. Gently pull on both yarn ends to tighten the knot. Then pull on the yarn leading to the ball of yarn to tighten the knot on the needle.

Casting on (cable method)

This method of casting on makes a firm edge and uses two needles. It is given for the English method of knitting here.

1 Make a slip knot as shown (left). Put the needle with the slip knot into your left hand. Insert the point of the other needle into the front of the slip knot and under the left needle. Wind the yarn from the ball of yarn around the tip of the right needle.

2 Using the tip of the needle, draw the yarn through the slip knot to form a loop. This loop is the new stitch. Slip the loop from the right-hand needle onto the left-hand needle.

3 To make the next stitch, insert the tip of the right-hand needle between the two stitches. Wind the yarn over the right needle, from left to right, then draw the yarn through to form a loop. Transfer this loop to the left-hand needle. Repeat until you have cast on the right number of stitches for the project.

Casting on (long tail method)

This method produces a neat, even edge that is suitable for projects that begin with a section of ribbing.

1 Pull out a long tail of yarn, then make a slip knot and put it onto a needle, holding this needle in your dominant hand. Hold your other hand with the palm facing toward you, and wind the long tail of yarn around your thumb in a counterclockwise direction. Pass the other end of the yarn (attached to the ball) over your index finger, as shown. Trap both the strands in place under your third and little finger.

2 Insert your needle under the horizontal strand of yarn that is on the outside of your thumb.

3 Now guide the needle over and then under the strand attached to your index finger, as shown.

4 Bring the needle back through the center of the loop around your thumb to make the stitch.

5 Remove your thumb from the loop and tighten up the stitch by pulling on the long tail. Reposition the yarn around your thumb, as in step 1, and repeat these steps for each cast on stitch.

Knit stitch

There are only two stitches to master in knitting; knit stitch and purl stitch. Most people in the English-speaking world knit using a method called English (or American) knitting. However, in parts of Europe people prefer a method known as Continental knitting.

Knit US/UK style

1 Hold the needle with the cast-on stitches in your left hand, and then insert the point of the right-hand needle into the front of the first stitch from left to right. Wind the yarn around the point of the right-hand needle, from left to right.

2 With the tip of the right-hand needle, pull the yarn through the stitch to form a loop. This loop is the new stitch.

3 Slip the original stitch off the left-hand needle by gently pulling the right-hand needle to the right. Repeat these steps until you have knitted all the stitches on the left-hand needle. To work the next row, transfer the needle with all the stitches into your left hand.

Knit Continental style

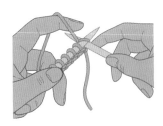

1 Hold the needle with the stitches to be knitted in your left hand, and then insert the tip of the right-hand needle into the front of the first stitch from left to right. Holding the yarn fairly taut with your left hand at the back of your work, use the tip of the right-hand needle to pick up a loop of yarn.

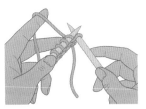 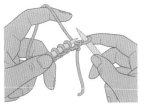

2 With the tip of the right-hand needle, bring the yarn through the original stitch to form a loop. This loop is the new stitch.

3 Slip the original stitch off the left-hand needle by gently pulling the right-hand needle to the right. Repeat these steps until you have knitted all the stitches on the left-hand needle. To work the next row, transfer the needle with all the stitches into your left hand.

Purl stitch

As with knit stitch, purl stitch can be formed in two ways. If you are new to knitting, try both techniques to see which works better for you: left-handed people may find the Continental method easier to master.

Purl US/UK style

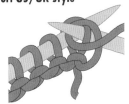  

1 Hold the needle with the stitches in your left hand, and then insert the point of the right-hand needle into the front of the first stitch from right to left. Wind the yarn around the point of the right-hand needle, from right to left.

2 With the tip of the right-hand needle, pull the yarn through the stitch to form a loop. This loop is the new stitch.

3 Slip the original stitch off the left-hand needle by gently pulling the right-hand needle to the right. Repeat these steps until you have purled all the stitches on the left-hand needle. To work the next row, transfer the needle with all the stitches into your left hand.

Purl Continental style

1 Hold the needle with the stitches to be knitted in your left hand, and then insert the tip of the right-hand needle into the front of the first stitch from right to left. Holding the yarn fairly taut at the front of the work, move the tip of the right-hand needle under the working yarn, then push your left index finger downward, as shown, to hold the yarn around the needle.

2 With the tip of the right-hand needle, bring the yarn through the original stitch to form a loop.

3 Slip the original stitch off the left-hand needle by gently pulling the right-hand needle to the right. Repeat these steps till you have purled all the stitches on the left-hand needle. To work the next row, transfer the needle with all the stitches into your left hand.

Binding (casting) off

You need to bind (cast) off the stitches to complete the projects and stop the knitting unraveling.

1 First knit two stitches in the normal way. With the point of the left-hand needle, pick up the first stitch you have just knitted and lift it over the second stitch. Knit another stitch so that there are two stitches on the right-hand needle again. Repeat the process of lifting the first stitch over the second stitch. Continue this process until there is just one stitch remaining on the right-hand needle.

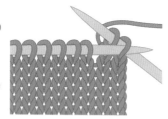

2 Break the yarn, leaving a tail of yarn long enough to sew the work together (see page 124). Pull the tail all the way through the last stitch. Slip the stitch off the needle and pull it fairly tightly to make sure it is secure.

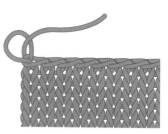

Slipping stitches

This means moving stitches from one needle to the other without knitting or purling them.
They can be slipped knitwise or purlwise, but unless stated otherwise in a pattern, slip them purlwise.

Knitwise

From left to right, put the right-hand needle into the next stitch on the left-hand needle (as shown by the arrow) and slip it across onto the right-hand needle without working it.

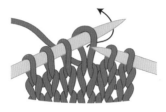

Purlwise

You can slip a stitch purlwise on a purl row or a knit row. From right to left, put the right-hand needle into the next stitch on the left-hand needle and slip it across onto the right-hand needle without working it.

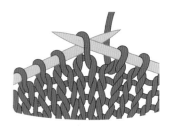

Yarnover (yo)

To make a yarnover you wind the yarn around the right-hand needle to make an extra loop that is worked as a stitch on the next row. Winding the yarn around twice creates a double yarnover (yo twice).

Bring the yarn between the tips of the needles to the front. Take the yarn over the right-hand needle to the back and knit the next stitch on the left-hand needle (see page 117).

Note that in the UK this is called "yarn forward" and is abbreviated to "yfwd."

Increasing

There are three methods of increasing used in projects in this book.

Increase on a knit row (kfb)

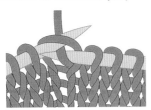 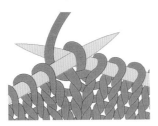 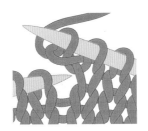

1 Knit the next stitch on the left-hand needle in the usual way (see page 117), but do not slip the "old" stitch off the left-hand needle.

2 Move the right-hand needle behind the left-hand needle and put it into the same stitch again, but through the back of the stitch this time. Knit the stitch again.

3 Now slip the "old" stitch off the left-hand needle in the usual way.

Increase on a purl row (inc pwise)

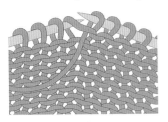 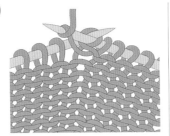

1 Purl the next stitch on the left-hand needle in the usual way (see page 117), but do not slip the "old" stitch off the left-hand needle.

2 Twist the right-hand needle backward to make it easier to put it into the same stitch again, but through the back of the stitch this time. Purl the stitch again, then slip the "old" stitch off the left-hand needle in the usual way.

Make one stitch (m1)

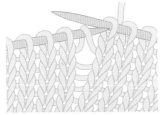 

1 From the front, slip the tip of the left-hand needle under the horizontal strand of yarn running between the last stitch on the right-hand needle and the first stitch on the left-hand needle.

2 Put the right-hand needle knitwise into the back of the loop formed by the picked-up strand and knit into it in the normal way. (It is important to knit into the back of the loop so that it is twisted and a hole does not form in your work.)

Decreasing

There are five different ways of decreasing used in this book, one of which decreases by two stitches rather than one stitch.

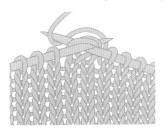 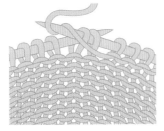 

Knit two together (k2tog)
This is the simplest way of decreasing. Simply insert the right-hand needle through two stitches instead of the normal one, and then knit them in the usual way.

Purl two together (p2tog)
To make a simple decrease on a purl row, insert the right-hand needle through two stitches instead of the normal one, and then purl them in the usual way.

Knit three stitches together (k3tog)
Worked exactly the same way as k2tog, except that you insert your right needle into three stitches rather than two, and knit them all together as if they were one stitch.

Slip, slip, knit (ssk)

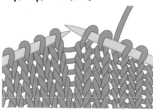 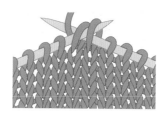

1 Slip one stitch knitwise (see page 118), and then the next stitch knitwise onto the right-hand needle, without knitting them.

2 Insert the left-hand needle from left to right through the front loops of both the slipped stitches and knit them in the usual way.

Slip one, knit two together, pass the slipped stitch over (sk2po)

Reduce the number of stitches by two using this decrease.

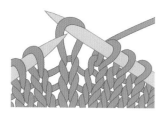 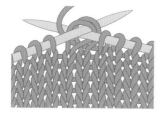 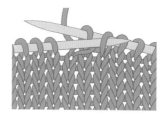

1 Slip the first stitch knitwise from the left-hand to the right-hand needle (see page 118).

2 Knit the next two stitches on the left-hand needle together (see page 119).

3 Lift the slipped stitch over the knitted stitch and drop it off the needle.

Knitting in the round

Circular needle

These needles have short straight tips that are joined with a nylon cable. As well as the usual needle size information, the pattern will tell you what length of needle you need so that your stitches fit on it without stretching.

1 Cast on the number of stitches needed; just ignore the cable connecting the two tips and cast on the stitches as if you were using two separate needles. Spread out the cast-on row along the length of the cable and make sure that it is not twisted or you will end up with a twist in the knitting.

2 Simply knit the stitches from the right-hand tip onto the left-hand tip sliding them around the cable as you work. The first stitch is the beginning of the round, so place a round marker on the needle to keep track of the rounds. When you get back to the marker, you have completed one round. Slip the marker onto the right-hand tip of the needle and knit the next round.

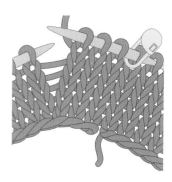

Double-pointed needles (DPNs)

If you do not have enough stitches to stretch around a circular needle (see page 120), then you need to work on double-pointed needles. This is one of those knitting techniques that looks terrifying, but isn't actually that hard to do; you just ignore all the needles other than the two you are working with. Double-pointed needles—usually called "DPNS"—come in sets of four or five and a pattern will tell you how many you need.

1 Divide evenly into three (if using four needles), or into four (if using five needles), the number of stitches you need to cast on. Here, a set of four needles is being used. Cast on (see page 116) to one needle one-third of the number of stitches needed, plus one extra stitch. Slip the extra stitch onto the second needle. Repeat the process, not forgetting to count the extra stitch, until the right number of stitches is cast on to each of the needles.

2 Arrange the needles in a triangle with the tips overlapping as shown here. As with circular knitting (see page 120) make sure that the cast-on edge is not twisted and place a round marker to keep track of the rounds. Pull the working tail of yarn across from the last stitch and using the free needle, knit the first stitch off the first needle (see page 117), knitting it firmly and pulling the yarn tight. Knit the rest of the stitches on the first needle, which then becomes the free one, ready to knit the stitches off the second needle. Knit the stitches off each needle in turn; when you get back to the marker, you have completed one round. Slip the marker onto the next needle and knit the next round.

Cables

This is another technique that looks difficult, but really isn't. All you are doing is moving groups of stitches using a cable needle. Work a six-stitch cable as shown here: if it is a four stitch cable, then slip two stitches onto the needle and knit two, rather than three. For an eight-stitch cable, slip four stitches onto the needle and knit four; and for a ten-stitch cable, slip five stitches onto the needle and knit five.

Cable six front

This cable twists to the left and is abbreviated to "C6F" in a knitting pattern.

1 Work to the position of the cable. Slip the next three stitches on the left-hand needle purlwise (see page 118) onto the cable needle, then leave the cable needle in front of the work.

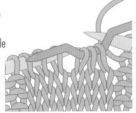

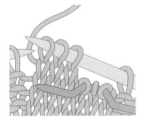

2 Knit the next three stitches off the left-hand needle in the usual way (see page 118).

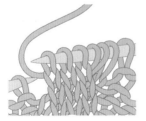

3 Then knit three stitches off the cable needle. The cable is completed.

Cable six back

This cable twists to the right and is abbreviated to "C6B" in a knitting pattern.

1 Work to the position of the cable. Slip the next three stitches on the left-hand needle purlwise (see page 118) onto the cable needle, then leave the cable needle at the back of the work.

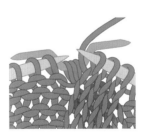

2 Knit the next three stitches of the left-hand needle in the usual way (see page 118).

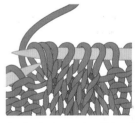

3 Then knit the three stitches off the cable needle. The cable is completed.

Knitting in different colors

It's important to change colors in the right way to keep the knitted fabric flat and smooth and without any holes or gaps.

Stranding

If you are knitting just a few stitches in a different color, you can simply leave the color you are not using on the wrong side of the work and pick it up again when you need to.

Changing color on a knit row

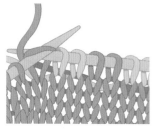 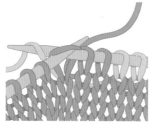

1 Knit the stitches (see page 117) in color A (brown in this example), bringing the yarn across over the strand of color B (lime in this example) to wrap around the needle.

2 At the color change, drop color A and pick up color B, bringing it across under the strand of color A to wrap around the needle. Be careful not to pull it too tight. Knit the stitches in color B. When you change back to color A, bring it across over the strand of color B.

Changing color on a purl row

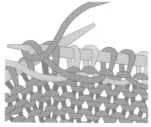 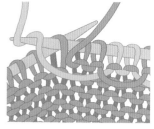

1 Purl the stitches (see page 117) in color A (brown in this example), bringing it across over the strand of color B (lime in this example) to wrap around the needle.

2 At the color change, drop color A and pick up color B, bringing it across under the strand of color A to wrap around the needle. Be careful not to pull it too tight. Purl the stitches in color B. When you change back to color A, bring it across over the strand of color B.

Intarsia

If you are knitting blocks of different colors within a project then you will need to use a technique called intarsia. This involves having separate balls of yarn for each area and twisting the yarns together where they join to avoid creating a hole or gap.

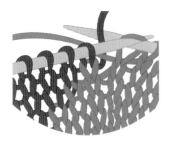 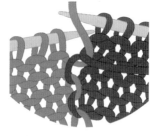

On the right side

When you want to change colors and the color change is vertical or sloping to the right, take the first color over the second color. Then pick up the second color, so the strands of yarn cross each other.

On the wrong side

On this side it is easy to see how the yarns must be interlinked at each color change.

This is worked in almost the same way as on the right side. When you want to change colors and the color change is vertical or sloping to the left, take the first color over the second color. Then pick up the second color, so the strands of yarn cross each other.

Blocking

If, once you have finished a piece of knitting, it doesn't look as smooth as you hoped it would, then blocking it can help. You can also use this process to straighten or to re-shape pieces a little if need be. The precise method of blocking you use depends on the fiber the yarn is spun from: the ball band will give you advice on that.

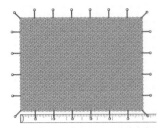
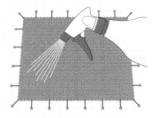
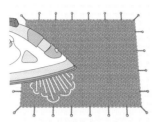

1 Lay the piece of knitting flat on an ironing board and ease it into shape. Don't pull hard and keep the knitting flat. Starting at the corners (if there are any), pin the edges of the piece to the ironing board, pushing the pins in far enough to hold the knitting firmly. Use a ruler or tape measure to check that the pinned pieces are the right size.

2 If the fiber or texture of your yarn does not respond well to heat, then you will need to wet block it. Use a spray bottle of cold water to completely dampen the knitting, but do not make it soaking wet. Leave the knitting to dry naturally, then unpin it.

3 If you can use heat, then set the iron to the temperature the yarn ball band recommends. Hold the iron 1in (2.5cm) above the surface of the knitting and steam it for a couple of minutes. Move the iron so that the whole surface gets steamed, but don't actually touch the knitting with the iron as this can spoil the texture and drape of the fabric and may leave shiny patches. Leave the knitting to dry naturally, then unpin it.

Weaving in yarn tails/ends

You will need a blunt-ended darning needle with a large eye—these are sometimes called "knitter's needles" or "yarn needles" and are often sold in pairs, one large and one smaller. A blunt-ended needle will not split the stitches into individual strands as you sew, which would make sewing much more difficult and produce a weak, untidy seam. You will also need small, sharp scissors.

Take a yarn end and thread it into the needle. With the wrong side of the work facing you, follow along one row of horizontal stitch "bars"—this might be on the last/first row, or in the middle of the piece; wherever the yarn tail occurs, work in the row alongside it. Sew up and down through this row, working the yarn in and out so that it snakes through the stitches, as shown above. Work about 4in (10cm) of the tail in, and then trim off close to the work.

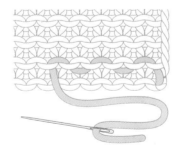

Sewing seams

There are various ways to join pieces of knitting, and the patterns advise you on which stitch to use.

Mattress stitch on row-end edges

1 Right-sides up, lay the two edges to be joined side by side. Thread a yarn sewing needle with a tail left after binding (casting) off, or a long length of yarn.

From the back bring the needle up between the first and second stitches of the left-hand piece, immediately above the cast-on edge. Take it across to the right-hand piece, and from the back bring it through between the first and second stitches of that piece, immediately above the cast-on edge. Take it back to the left-hand piece and, again from the back, bring it through one row above where it first came through, between the first and second stitches. Pull the yarn through and this figure–eight will hold the cast-on edges level.

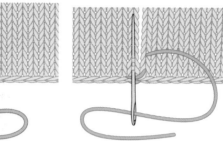

2 Take the needle across to the right-hand piece and, from the front, take it under the bars of yarn between the first and second stitches on the next two rows up. Take the needle across to the left-hand piece and, from the front, take it under the bars of yarn between the first and second stitches on the next two rows up.

3 Repeat Step 2 to sew up the seam. When you have sewn about 1in (2.5cm), gently and evenly pull the stitches tight to close the seam, and then continue.

Flat stitch

Unlike mattress stitch, this stitch creates a join that is completely flat.

Lay the two edges to be joined side by side with the right side facing you. Using a yarn sewing needle, pick up the very outermost strand of knitting from one side and then the other, working your way along the seam and pulling your yarn up firmly every few stitches.

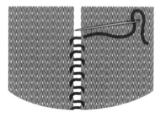

Oversewing

This stitch can be worked with the right or the wrong sides of the work together. Take the yarn from the front of the work, over the edge of the seam, and out through the front again a short distance further on.

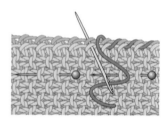

Grafting

This is also called Kitchener stitch. Arrange the two needles parallel with one another.

1 Measure out the working yarn to four times the width of the knitting, cut the yarn, and thread a blunt-ended or knitter's sewing needle. From the back, bring the sewing needle through the first stitch of the lower piece and then, from the front, through the first stitch of the upper piece. Take the needle through the second stitch of the upper piece from the back, then from the front back through the first stitch of the lower piece. Bring it back to the front through the second stitch of the lower piece.

Continue in this pattern across the row, taking the sewing needle through a stitch from the front and then through the adjacent stitch on the same piece from the back. Take the needle across to the other piece of knitting and take it from the front through the stitch it last came out of, then through the back of the adjacent stitch on the same piece. Slide the knitting needles out of the knitted stitches as you join them.

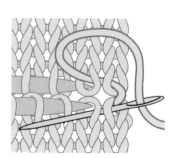

Picking up stitches

For some projects, you will need to pick up stitches along either a horizontal edge (the cast-on or bound-/cast-off edge of your knitting), or a vertical edge (the edges of your rows of knitting).

Along a row-end edge

With the right side of the knitting facing you, insert a knitting needle from the front to back between the first and second stitches of the first row. Wind the yarn around the needle and pull through a loop to form the new stitch. Normally you have more gaps between rows than stitches you need to pick up and knit. To make sure your picking up is even, you will have to miss a gap every few rows.

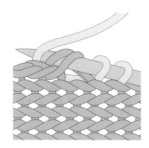

Along a cast-on or bound- (cast-) off edge

This is worked in the same way as picking up stitches along a vertical edge, except that you will work through the cast-on stitches rather than the gaps between rows. You will normally have the same number of stitches to pick up and knit as there are existing stitches.

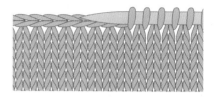

Sewing stitches

Duplicate stitch (Swiss darning)

Also known as Swiss darning, this is a useful technique to learn. Not only is it a very effective way to embellish your work, it can also be used to cover up small mistakes in colorwork patterns or to repair threadbare or damaged knitting. Swiss darning is more effective when worked on the knit side of stockinette (stocking) stitch, but it can be worked on purl stitches once you have learned the method. Essentially the technique is very simple, because you are following the path of the knitted stitch beneath.

To practice this technique, work up a small piece of plain stockinette (stocking) stitch and then duplicate stitch a horizontal line in another color, or try working a small motif such as a simple cross or diamond.

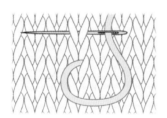

1 Thread up a blunt-ended needle with a length of contrast yarn. With the RS of the knitted piece facing you, insert the needle into the back of the work and bring it out at the front, at the base of the V of the stitch to embroider over. Pass the needle behind both bars of the V of the stitch above the one you are working on, and pull the yarn through.

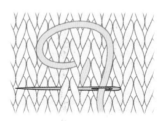

2 Insert the needle back into the space where you began the stitch, at the base of the knitted V you have covered.

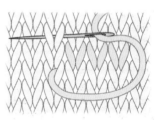

3 Try to work from right to left, as shown here, because the sewing will be imitating the natural path of the knitted row beneath. Finish off your loose yarn tails by weaving them in as normal.

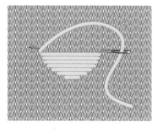

Satin stitch

Work parallel stitches, close together, bringing the needle up and taking it down through the knitted fabric on the edges of the design. Do not pull the thread tightly or you will distort the fabric.

Blanket stitch

1 Bring the needle through at the edge of the fabric. Push the needle back through the fabric a short distance from the edge and loop the thread under the needle. Pull the needle and thread as far as you can to make the first stitch.

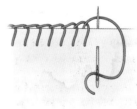

2 Make another stitch to the right of this and again loop the thread under the needle. Continue along the fabric and finish with a few small stitches or a knot on the underside.

Basic crochet

Crochet chain

While the projects in this book are all knitted rather than crocheted, a few of them require simple crochet stitches.

 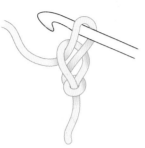

1 Make a slip knot on the crochet hook in the same way as for knitting (see page 116). Holding the slip stitch on the hook, wind the yarn over round the hook from the back to the front, then catch the yarn in the crochet-hook tip.

2 Pull the yarn through the slip stitch on the crochet hook to make the second link in the chain. Continue in this way till the chain is the length needed.

US single crochet (sc)/UK double crochet (dc)

Note: US single crochet (sc) = UK double crochet (dc)

1 Insert the hook into your work, yarn over/round hook and pull the yarn through the work only. You will then have 2 loops on the hook.

2 Yarn over/round hook again and pull through the two loops on the hook. You will then have 1 loop on the hook.

Crochet slip stitch
Slip stitch (sl st)

A slip stitch doesn't create any height and is often used as the last stitch to create a smooth and even round or row.

1 To make a slip stitch: first put the hook through the work, yarn over/round hook.

2 Pull the yarn through both the work and the loop on the hook at the same time, so you will have 1 loop on the hook.

abbreviations

DPN	Double-pointed needles
k	Knit
k2tog	Knit 2 stitches together (decrease 1)
k3tog	Knit 3 stitches together (decrease 2)
kfb	Knit into the front then back of one stitch (increase 1)
psso	Pass slipped stitch over
pm	Place marker
p	Purl
p2tog	Purl 2 stitches together (decrease 1)
p3tog	Purl 2 stitches together (decrease 2)
rep	Repeat
RS	Right side
sl	Slip
skpo	Slip 1 stitch, knit next stitch, pass slipped stitch over the knitted stitch (decrease 1)
sm	Slip marker
ssk	Slip 1 stitch knitwise, slip the next stitch knitwise, knit both these stitches together through the back loop (decrease 1)
st(s)	Stitch(es)
st st	Stockinette (stocking) stitch
WS	Wrong side
yo	Yarn over needle

yarn suppliers

There is a strong tendency to lean toward the purest and most natural of fibers when it comes to baby knits, and gradually introduce more easy-care yarns through the toddler years.

The makes featured in this book have been created using a wide range of yarns in varied colorways, fibers, and styles—here are some brands whose yarns have been featured in the makes in this book and suggested online suppliers and retailers:

Aracunia
www.knittingfever.com
www.designeryarns.uk.com

Bernat
www.yarnspirations.com
www.deramores.com

Berroco
www.berroco.com
www.loveknitting.com

Brown Sheep Company
www.brownsheep.com
www.loveknitting.com

Cascade
www.cascadeyarns.com
www.deramores.com

Debbie Bliss
www.designeryarns.uk.com
www.knittingfever.com
www.deramores.com

Fyberspates
www.fyberspates.co.uk
www.fyberspatesusa.com

Lion Brand
www.lionbrand.com
www.deramores.com

MillaMia
www.deramores.com
www.millamia.com

Mirasol
www.knittingfever.com
www.designeryarns.uk.com

Red Heart Soft
www.redheart.com
www.loveknitting.com

Rowan
www.knitrowan.com
www.jimmybeanswool.com

For tools and finishings, the following have store locators on their websites, as well as online sales:

US
Jo-Ann Fabric and Craft Stores
www.joann.com

Michaels
www.michaels.com

WEBS
www.yarn.com

UK
Hobbycraft
www.hobbycraft.co.uk

John Lewis
www.johnlewis.com

index

acknowledgements

I must first give thanks to the fabulous support of a number of yarn companies that have provided some of the wonderful yarns that have gone into these projects—Brown Sheep Company, Cascade Yarns, Rowan & Designer Yarns—because every knitter dreams of starting out a collection with such a fabulous stash of yarns!

Thank you to Cindy Richards, Penny Craig, Miriam Catley, Rachel Atkinson, Jemima Bicknell, and all of the team at CICO, who have once again created a stunning book that I am so proud to be part of.

To my online friends and readers of www.madepeachy.com, thank you for your continued support and I hope you love this new book too!

My family and friends, especially my dear friend Louise Kelly, are a continual source of support and encouragement—and never of tire hearing about all the ups and downs of creating a knitting collection. Last, but never least, my never ending thanks to my husband John, for helping me to chase every single dream!